"Once again, Del Duduit knocks it out of the park. After many years of writing sports devotions, Del brings these fantastic stories to kids. *Sports Shorts* is adapted in a language and fashion that kids can relate to their everyday lives. Reading these devotions will help your youngster be an All-Star Believer."
—**Billie Jauss**, speaker, host of *start small BELIEVE BIG* podcast and author of *Distraction Detox* and *Making Room*

"Del has a unique way of getting those powerful quotes from the athletes we admire and turning those thoughts into a faith-based, interesting lesson for kids. From learning how to stick with something even when it's difficult to trusting God's timing in all things, this book will truly help children grow closer to God. Each of the 52 devotions features 'The Big Moment,' which poses thought-provoking questions; 'The Big Play,' which drives home the point of the devotion; and 'The Coach's Corner,' which offers that all-important takeaway and related scripture verse. Bottom line, this book is a winner! I can't wait to share it with all of the children in my world."
—**Michelle Medlock Adams**, multi-award-winning author of more than 100 books, including *Dinosaur Devotions* and *Get Your Spirit On*

"This is a captivating read for the younger generation. It teaches them that struggles happen, but God will be there to guide them every step of the way. Del uses inspirational stories of sports stars to help kids recognize the power of faith in their lives."
—**Caris Snider**, author, speaker, certified professional life coach

"In *Sports Shorts*, award-winning author Del Duduit shows his talent to tell the story that has a deeper impact. Each devotion connects with young readers and promis⸱ ⸱⸱⸱⸱⸱ ⸱⸱⸱⸱⸱ ⸱⸱⸱⸱⸱ ⸱⸱⸱⸱⸱. This book is guaranteed to advance the g⸱ ⸱⸱⸱⸱⸱ ⸱⸱⸱⸱⸱ ⸱⸱⸱⸱⸱ ⸱⸱⸱⸱⸱ stories of champions on the fie⸱ ⸱⸱⸱⸱⸱

and leaders. As a pastor, this resource will be used at our church and should be used in churches throughout America."
—**Andy Clapp**, award-winning author of *Midnight, Christmas Eve*

"Del Duduit knocks it out of the park with 52 brief yet powerful lessons for kids as inspired by some of the greatest contemporary sports giants in the country. At a time when kids idolize big names in sports, why not encourage them to admire those who profess Jesus as their Savior and give God the glory for their accomplishments? Each chapter features stories and quotes from successful athletes and then wraps up with thoughts and suggestions to help kids apply the spiritual lesson to their own lives. Every youngster needs a copy of *Sports Shorts* for the win!"
—**Julie Lavender**, author of *365 Ways to Love Your Child* and *Children's Bible Stories for Bedtime*

Other books in the Stars of the Faith Series

Dugout Devotions: Inspirational Hits from MLB's Best
Dugout Devotions II: More Inspirational Hits from MLB's Best
First Down Devotions: Inspiration from NFL's Best
First Down Devotions II: More Inspiration from NFL's Best
Auburn Believer: 40 Days of Devotions for the Tiger Faithful
Alabama Believer: 40 Days of Devotions for the Roll Tide Faithful

SPORTS SHORTS

52 STORIES OF FAITH FROM ALL-STAR BELIEVERS

DEL DUDUIT

IRON STREAM KIDS

Birmingham, Alabama

Sports Shorts

Iron Stream Kids
An imprint of Iron Stream Media
100 Missionary Ridge
Birmingham, AL 35242
IronStreamMedia.com

Published in association with Cyle Young of
the Hartline Literary Agency, LLC.

Library of Congress Control Number: 2021950068

Cover design by Jonlin Creative

ISBN: 978-1-56309-548-1 (paperback)
ISBN: 978-1-56309-549-8 (e-book)

1 2 3 4 5—26 25 24 23 22

This book is dedicated to my grandson Lawson.

My granddaughter has an unmatched vibrant personality, and my other grandson is just plain adorable.

But you, Lawson, have to be the sweetest little person I've ever met. You are unique.

The first time I held you soon after you were born, I just knew it. You melted into my arms and when you opened your precious eyes you had to sweetest look on your tiny and innocent face.

I know you will be in good hands. Your dad is the most passionate person I know, and your mom will dedicate her life to you.

And you will fit right in with the other grandkids, but you'll have to hold your own. I am confident you will accomplish this task and anything you put your mind to. As your papaw, I promise to be there and support you no matter what you want to accomplish. I will love you without condition and will try to be a positive example.

At some point in your life, you will have the opportunity to serve God, and I hope you accept this challenge. And as long as you keep that sweet and pleasant personality, you will be a beacon of light and hope to everyone you meet. You already inspire me. My prayers and desires are that this book will snuggle its way into your life at some point and that you will take the time to read the words and hide them in your heart.

You will always be precious to me.

Papaw

CONTENTS

ACKNOWLEDGMENTS

The following people played a big part in this book becoming a reality, and I want to extend my sincere appreciation to:

My wife, Angie, for being my first editor and constant support.

My agent, Cyle Young, for your trust and belief in me.

My publisher, John Herring, for this wonderful opportunity.

My editors, Ramona Richards and Susan Cornell, for making this book much better.

My friend and colleague, Michelle Medlock Adams, for the inspiration for the title and for guiding me in my first children's book.

My colleague Jacob Smith at the *Portsmouth Daily Times* for assistance in media credentials.

My Lord and Savior for your forgiveness and unconditional love.

FOREWORD

Little did I know when I answered a message on LinkedIn a little over five years ago that I'd be gaining a valued colleague, a future coauthor, and a trusted friend. (I always refer to Del Duduit as the brother I never wanted, LOL. But in all seriousness, I can't imagine my writing world without Del and his lovely wife, Angie, in it.)

Del reached out, asking how I had made the jump from newspaper writing to the world of writing books, seeing that our professional backgrounds were so similar—both beginning our careers as sportswriters for daily newspapers. We ended up chatting for over an hour that day, and I told him four things he needed to do in order to jumpstart his publishing career: get a writer's website to highlight his work, sign up for the Florida Christian Writers Conference that was coming up, put together some book proposals for that conference, and begin building his social media platform.

Here's the thing. I've given many writers that same advice over the years, and most of them have never acted on even one of my directives, so imagine my surprise when Del reached back out a few weeks later and had already signed up for the FCWC, put together a few proposals, developed a writer's website, and was actively building his social media presence. I was impressed, and I continue to be impressed by Del's work ethic and talent. I often refer to his unbelievable ability to get the big interviews when I teach at various writers conferences and universities.

He's the guy who can get an interview with professional athletes that other reporters only dream of, which is why he was the perfect person to write this book, *Sports Shorts: 52 Stories of Faith from All-Star Believers*. I love this book so much, and I know kids will love it too. I say that not only as a friend of Del's but also as the author of many award-winning children's books. Del has a unique way of getting those powerful quotes from the athletes we admire and turning those thoughts into a faith-based, interesting lesson for kids. From learning how to stick with something even when it's difficult to trusting God's timing in all things, this book will truly help children grow closer to God. Each of the fifty-two devotions features "The Big Moment," which poses thought-provoking questions, "The Big Play," which drives home the point of the devotion, and "The Coach's Corner," which offers that all-important takeaway and related scripture verse. Bottom line, this book is a winner! I can't wait to share it with all of the children in my world.

Encouraging children to have their own one-on-one time with God is so important, and this book is sure to make that special time with God even more enjoyable and beneficial. As parents and grandparents, aunts and uncles, and caregivers, we love to give good gifts to our kiddos, and I can't think of a better gift than *Sports Shorts*.

Michelle Medlock Adams

CHAPTER 1
A REASON TO SMILE

Francisco Lindor
MLB All-Star Shortstop

Do you smile? What puts a big grin on your face?

The shortstop for the New York Mets has a big reason to show his pearly whites.

Francisco always shows off a smile—even when he doesn't feel like it.

Do you know why he smiles all the time?

Because God has been good to him.

That doesn't mean he does not have problems. It means he knows that Jesus Christ will take care of him, no matter what comes his way.

"Life has not always been easy for me," he said. "I've had my struggles, but I learned early to completely turn things over to Him and wait. That's hard to do sometimes, but it's the best thing to do."

This is the main reason Francisco smiles.

It's not because he plays for the New York Mets or went to a World Series. He's not happy because he has played in All-Star games. Francisco does not smile because he makes a lot of money, or when he eats his favorite breakfast of chocolate chip pancakes.

He smiles because he is a Christian and is saved.

"I'm happy because God is in my heart," he said. "That's the most important thing. If I did not have faith and God in my life, I'd be in a bad place right now. I don't want to think about it really because it's scary not to have God."

When you see Francisco run onto a baseball diamond, you will notice that he hustles, plays hard, and always smiles.

The Big Moment

Are there situations in your life that make you sad? That's okay. Everyone has them. Maybe you received a bad grade in school or someone is bullying you. Perhaps you are sick a lot or don't have a lot of friends. It's okay to feel that way, but don't stay in that sad place for long. Tell someone you trust how you're feeling and tell God. You can talk to Him just like you talk to a friend. He is your friend.

The Big Play

Whenever you're unhappy, remember that God loves you and will take care of you. Read your Bible, pray, and wait for God to help you. Will you have problems? Yes. Will Jesus let you down? No. God will never let you down. You can trust Him, and that should put a big smile on your face.

The Coach's Corner

When you smile, like Francisco, your happiness will rub off on those around you. People like to be with others who are positive and in a good mood. Your friends will know you are a child of the King, and one day you will be in heaven on the biggest baseball field ever. Smile.

> *May the LORD smile on you and be gracious to you.*
> —Numbers 6:25

CHAPTER 2
DON'T QUIT TRYING

DeAndre Hopkins
NFL All-Pro Wide Receiver

Have you ever wanted to just quit? Quit school. Quit football or baseball. Quit being friends with certain people because they made you mad. You just want to quit.

There are a lot of things that can make you feel this way.

DeAndre Hopkins could have quit when a lot of bad things happened to him. But he refused to throw in the towel.

When he was just a few months old, his dad died in a car crash.

When DeAndre was ten years old, his mom was injured and lost sight in one of her eyes.

If that were not enough, a close uncle was killed.

His family was poor, and he lived in a rough neighborhood.

When he played football for Clemson, he was on his way to a big game and got knocked out in a car accident.

And there were more bad things that happened to DeAndre. He could have quit everything because he was sad and upset.

"We all have obstacles to overcome," he said. "I didn't complain, but life was tough for me back then."

But his mother made sure he went to church and Sunday school, where he learned to trust God during the rough times.

"I watched her faith grow stronger and stronger, and she showed me the importance of hard work and to trust the Man upstairs," DeAndre said. "And I never forgot that."

He could have quit, but he did not. He worked hard and made it to the NFL.

"You just keep working, live right, and have faith in the Lord," DeAndre said.

The Big Moment

Have you ever been bullied and wanted to quit school? Maybe you fumbled the football in a game and your team lost. Or perhaps someone told a lie about you, and some friends turned their backs on you. You will go through some tough times and struggles, but always know that God will not want you to quit on anything you start, especially church and Sunday school. Don't ever give up praying for your family and friends. Never give up.

The Big Play

DeAndre got through his tough times as a child. He stayed faithful to the Lord, who made it possible for him to play football in the NFL. Maybe someday you'll play football or baseball, and maybe not. But the best thing to do is to trust God for the plan He has for your life. Don't ever give up on yourself, your family, or Jesus.

The Coach's Corner

I coached young children in peewee football, Little League, and youth basketball. When players made a mistake, they sometimes wanted to quit. But you must learn from errors and have faith in yourself. Quitting should never be an option. Have faith in the Lord to get you through whatever problems you have.

But as for you, be strong and courageous, for your work will be rewarded.

—2 Chronicles 15:7

CHAPTER 3
ALWAYS TELL THE TRUTH

Andy Pettitte
MLB All-Star Pitcher

Is it okay to tell a little white lie? Have you ever stretched the truth a little bit?

Maybe you did something your parents asked you not to do, and now they want answers. Do you tell them the truth?

Or perhaps you told a fib to make yourself look good. Have you ever exaggerated details about something you did?

Or maybe you were about to get in trouble and told a lie to try to get out of the situation. Or maybe you kept a secret that you knew was wrong.

Andy Pettitte had this problem when he played for the New York Yankees.

He admitted that he took a substance to help his body get stronger after a surgery. At the time, it was not banned by Major League Baseball. So it was okay to take. But a few years later, league officials changed the rules, and this substance was no longer allowed.

But he felt bad anyway because some people might have thought he cheated when he didn't.

"I was having trouble sleeping at night," Andy said. "I needed to come clean with it."

Andy could have chosen not to tell his team and officials within the league that he took a substance that may have helped him gain an edge over the competition.

"It was during a time when nobody in the world would have known that I did it," he said. "But the Lord knew, and I knew."

He did the right thing by confessing. He could have kept the secret, but his conscience wouldn't let him.

Andy was respected and admired for telling the truth.

The Big Moment

Are you keeping a secret so you won't get in trouble? Maybe you cheated on a test or told a lie about someone. Or maybe you disobeyed your parents, and they don't know. Would you come clean and tell the truth, even if it means you get into trouble?

The Big Play

Honesty is not always easy. In fact, sometimes it's hard to do. When you try to cover up for a mistruth, things only get worse, and you start telling more lies. Then it becomes tough to remember all the lies you have already told. Life is so much simpler when you stick with the facts. You should always tell the truth.

The Coach's Corner

I talked to Andy about his confession, and he was sincere and meant what he said. He put his job and his reputation on the line when he told the truth. And he might have hurt his chances to get into the Hall of Fame. But that didn't matter. He thought it was more important to make sure God was happy with him.

And you will know the truth, and the truth will set you free.
—John 8:32

CHAPTER 4
FOLLOW GOOD EXAMPLES

Case Keenum
NFL Quarterback

Whom do you want to be like? Is there a teacher you admire, or an athlete you like to watch play on the field? Is there someone in your family you look to for advice?

Having a good role model is important, but you should always strive to be "you."

God made you in His image, and always remember there is no one quite like you.

But it's also important to have people with good morals and integrity in your life.

If you hang out with friends who get in trouble a lot or do things they should not do, then you need to get away from them.

Being cool is not always the best choice.

Quarterback Case Keenum liked to hang out with athletes who went to church and served God.

He thought that was the most important thing.

Case, whose favorite movie is *Remember the Titans*, was involved in Fellowship of Christian Athletes when he was young and admired the players who professed their faith in Christ.

"I wanted to throw the football like them, play like them, and talk like them," he said. "They had a big impact on me. It was the Christian athlete that really hit a chord with me."

He saw them put Jesus Christ first in their lives, and sports was second.

When he was in the third grade, Case became a Christian because of the impact these godly players had on his life.

The Big Moment

You might like to watch the best players on your favorite football teams. But are you still impressed with them if they say mean things on TV or get in trouble with the police? Maybe they were suspended for drug use or got into a fight with a referee. You might still want to watch them play ball, but do not pattern your life after them. Choose players who give God the glory when a victory is won.

The Big Play

There are many athletes who set good examples for kids. Case got involved with Fellowship of Christian Athletes, one of several Christian sports organizations that promote faith and character in athletes. These attributes are way more important than the touchdowns they score, or how many home runs they hit. It's about the lives they live in front of others that counts.

The Coach's Corner

Always remember to be you first. Never try to be like some-one else. You might try to replicate how Case throws a foot-ball and that's okay. He's pretty good at it. But watch how he treats people and what he says when he's interviewed. If he praises God on TV, then that is someone you want to be like. If he takes a knee to pray, then that is an action you want others to see. Case lets people know he loves God, and you should too.

Walk with the wise and become wise;
associate with fools and get in trouble.

—Proverbs 13:20

CHAPTER 5
TELL THE GOOD NEWS

Aaron Judge
MLB All-Star Outfielder

Do you tell others about God's grace? Do you use your social media to share about God's love?

If you have a social media account, you probably enjoy posting pictures of your pets or of vacation fun with family and friends. Everyone loves cool pictures of you at the beach.

But you can also use it to tell all your friends about the Lord.

Aaron Judge does it, and you can too.

If you follow baseball, you know that Aaron loves to blast home runs. He also enjoys telling others about his faith. He uses his social media account to proclaim his love for Jesus, and he's not ashamed of it.

"Any way I can spread the Word of God and get the message out there is a wonderful thing," he said. "I feel that is why I am where I am today."

He is happy to tell everyone he loves Jesus, and that he loves to play baseball. He also loves to eat pancakes and biscuits with gravy for breakfast.

He puts his priorities in perspective and always places God first. "If I go 0-4 at the plate, it's still a great day for me because I play for the best organization in baseball, and I'm a child of the King," he said.

God wants you to have fun and enjoy being a kid. But He also wants you to tell all your friends about Him in some way. Sometimes the life you live in front of them tells the story of God's love. You might just help a friend who is searching for happiness become a Christian.

The Big Moment

Do your friends know you love God? Do your teammates know you are a Christian? If they saw your social media profile, would they know you believe in Jesus? If not, does this mean you are afraid to tell them?

The Big Play

If you have a social media account, you can use it to let your followers know that you love God and your church. You can still post pictures of your kitten and your favorite snacks. But consider posting on your profile where you go to church and how you love Jesus. Aaron does it, and you can too.

The Coach's Corner

Social media can be a great way to be a Christian witness to your friends. Post a lesson you really liked from Sunday school, or pictures from church camp or vacation Bible school. Stand in the batter's box and smack a home run for

God. Don't be afraid to share your testimony. Be a social media Christian.

> *Everyone who acknowledges me publicly here on earth, I will also acknowledge before my Father in heaven.*
> —Matthew 10:32

CHAPTER 6
YOU MAKE THE CHOICE

RG3
NFL Pro-Bowl Quarterback

It's fun to have a choice.

When you go to a restaurant, you can order what you want. When your parents take you to an amusement park, you can select the rides you want to jump on for fun. For the most part, you can choose your friends.

Then there are times when you don't have much of a choice. If you want to drive a car, you will have to take a test. If you want to graduate from high school, you have to work for it.

But there is one aspect of your life where you—and only you—can make the right decision. Your parents and friends cannot make it for you.

You can choose to follow the Lord and become a Christian.

Robert Griffin III, or RG3 to his friends, said his parents took him to church and made sure he was around the right friends. But, eventually, he had to decide if he wanted to know Jesus as his Savior for himself.

"At a certain age, you have to make the decision on your own if you want to follow God or not. For me, I made the decision when I was about thirteen, but I wasn't really tested until I was eighteen years old."

Serving God does not mean you will never have any problems. It means you have a higher power on your side to help you through the tough times—just like He was for RG3.

When he was in college, he faced a few tough challenges, but he leaned on the Lord to help him through.

"I came out of those times stronger than ever in my faith," he said. "It was the first time I had to make the decision to follow God as a man."

The Big Moment

Have you made the decision to follow God? If you have done this, you already found out what a great move this was and have enjoyed the peace and happiness it brings. If you have not yet followed Christ, then you can choose today to become a believer. No one can do it for you—not your friends, pastors, or Sunday school teachers.

The Big Play

If you want to become a Christian, pray to Jesus and tell Him you are sorry for your sins. Ask Him to forgive you and to live inside your heart. Ask Him to guide your steps and put the right people in your life to help you along the way.

The Coach's Corner

If you have questions about becoming a Christian, seek out a believer to find out more information. Maybe this is a parent, pastor, Sunday school teacher, or just a friend who serves God. Make it your choice. And when you decide, it will be the best decision you will ever make.

For this is how God loved the world: He gave his one and only Son, so that everyone who believes in him will not perish but have eternal life.

—John 3:16

CHAPTER 7
FAITH IS HAPPINESS

José Altuve
MLB All-Star Second Baseman

Does having money make you successful? If you play for a baseball team that wins the World Series, does that make you a winner in life?

Some people might say yes, but money and accomplishments are not the true definition of success.

Perfect peace and happiness can only come through a genuine relationship with Jesus Christ.

Education and athletics are important, and you should always show up and do your best, but they are not as important as your belief in God.

José Altuve has won a World Series championship in baseball and is an All-Star player. His fans appreciate that he smiles and is always in a good mood.

He has won a Gold Glove, was named MVP of the American League, and has won several batting titles. No wonder he is happy. Right?

But all of these awards are not the real reason for his joy.

"Faith and your relationship with God does not happen because I am successful as a ball player," he said. "It doesn't work that way. It's easy for me to say this because I am playing baseball in the big leagues. But there were some times in my life when my family struggled."

Your faith and love for God should always be more important than any accomplishments in school or sports. As long as you put in the hard work and stay true to your heavenly Father, you will always be a winner in His eyes.

The Big Moment

Does your faith in God depend on your circumstances? Can you sing praises to Jesus when things aren't going your way? If you feel yucky and get upset about something that happened to you at school, will you trust Jesus to improve your situation?

The Big Play

The answers to all of those questions should be yes, yes, and yes. God is God no matter what you go through. He is God when you hit a home run, and He is God when you strike out.

The Coach's Corner

Kids today are influenced by some professional athletes who make a lot of money. They see pictures of fancy cars and big houses. But these things do not bring true happiness. José is happy that his teams have won, but the main reason he smiles is because Jesus is in his life.

Be happy with those who are happy, and weep with those who weep. Live in harmony with each other. Don't be too proud to enjoy the company of ordinary people. And don't think you know it all!

—Romans 12:15–16

CHAPTER 8
READ THE WORD

Teddy Bridgewater
NFL Pro Bowl Quarterback

When you get sad, or something happens to make you angry, how do you respond?

Do you find an object, throw it and cry, or scream at the top of your lungs? Most likely, your parents, coaches, and teachers would not approve.

But have you ever been so frustrated that you did not know how to act or what to do?

What do you think God wants you to do?

When Teddy Bridgewater gets upset or down, he likes to read the Bible and see what Jesus has to say to help him through the moment.

A long time ago, his mom was sick with cancer. She told Teddy to trust God and read His Word all the time.

"She told me to never give up hope and that no matter what, to always be happy and stay humble and smile," he said. "She always said that."

Teddy found hope and peace when he read the Bible every day. God's words made him feel happy.

"It doesn't matter the circumstance you face, there is a Bible verse to fit that need," he said. "There are different ones that apply to different occasions. But it's amazing that you can find one to fit any circumstance."

Instead of getting angry when something goes wrong, pick up God's Word and read some scripture. There is a good chance this will help you to feel better. And if you don't own one, download a free Bible app on your phone. Make a point to memorize some of your favorite verses to say to yourself when you need strength.

The Big Moment

Life can be tough. Maybe you got a bad grade, or your coach doesn't give you as much playing time as you wanted. Perhaps you had an argument with your best friend. No matter what the situation, there is a verse in the Bible to help you and give you peace.

The Big Play

Something good to practice is to control your attitude. When you become upset, notice the signs and step away for a few moments to pray. Then grab your phone and read a verse or two of scripture. This might not solve the problem, but it will help you handle it the right way.

The Coach's Corner

Find some favorite verses and memorize them to help you when you feel angry or sad. A verse can encourage you and help restore your confidence. Here are a couple suggestions:

Instead, be kind to each other, tenderhearted, forgiving one another, just as God through Christ has forgiven you.
                                                    —Ephesians 4:32

Do to others as you would like them to do to you.
                                                    —Luke 6:31

CHAPTER 9
GOD KNOWS YOU

Chris Davis
MLB All-Star First Baseman

One season, Chris Davis went through a rough slump where he had difficulty hitting the baseball, and he kept making outs.

This is a problem when it's your job to get hits, and you usually do it really well. In fact, he was so good at hitting home runs that he led the entire Major League in dingers twice.

His slump went on for many games, and fans started to get frustrated with Chris.

At one time, he went more than fifty-five times at bat without a hit.

People in the stands wondered if he would ever get a hit again. Some even booed him and urged his coach to bench him.

Even though some supporters of his team might have given up on Chris, God did not.

"There might be times when you feel like no one cares about you," he said. "But I know God cares deeply for me. He cares so much for me that He sent His Son to die for me."

That's big.

Chris knows that he plays baseball for a living, but his priority is Jesus. He loves the Lord, his family, and watching his favorite movie, *Forrest Gump*.

"He loves me even when I'm in a slump," Chris said. "If I get four hits in a game or none, He loves me. That is the best feeling in the world to know that God loves me no matter what."

Chris loves to eat pancakes, eggs, and bacon for breakfast. He also hangs with friends who think the way he does about God so they can help and encourage him.

"You have to surround yourself with good people who will help you," he said. "You can go to them with some problems and they can pray with you."

Slumps are not fun, but if you play baseball, you will probably experience one someday. The key is to keep stepping into the batter's box and don't give up.

The Big Moment

Have you ever been in a slump? Maybe yours does not relate to baseball. Maybe you've had times when you don't feel like serving God. Have you ever felt that way? For Chris, he said the best thing he did when he was in a baseball slump was to keep swinging.

The Big Play

You have to keep swinging the bat even though you may not feel like it. Keep praying, keep reading your Bible, and keep going to church. Trust God to give you the big hit to bring your team to victory.

The Coach's Corner

Chris doesn't feel like playing baseball all the time, but he does it because it's his job and because he loves it. He faces challenges but keeps showing up at the plate. Chris finally broke out of the slump. He didn't give up, and neither should you. Never give up on being the best Christian you can be.

So, my dear brothers and sisters, be strong and immovable. Always work enthusiastically for the Lord, for you know that nothing you do for the Lord is ever useless.
—1 Corinthians 15:58

CHAPTER 10
TREASURE YOUR BIBLE

Jarvis Landry
NFL Pro Bowl Wide Receiver

When you go on vacation, you pack what you need. If you are going to the beach, you might take your swimsuit, beach chairs, and towels.

If you are going to the mountains, you might pack some jackets as well as marshmallows, graham crackers, and chocolate to make s'mores. If you are going fishing for the weekend, you may pack fishing poles and buy some slimy worms.

The point is you should always be prepared when you take a trip. You never want to be caught off guard, especially if you go to the beach without sunscreen. Ouch.

When Jarvis Landry takes a business trip to play football on Sundays, he takes everything he needs. He packs his shoulder pads, his cleats, his helmet, and his uniform.

He also packs his Bible every time.

Jarvis not only knows the playbook for his football team but also reads God's playbook for his life.

"I keep it with me all the time," he said. "Especially when I go on the road. It's a sense of comfort for me. It just makes me feel better knowing I have it with me."

He received a Bible as a gift from a friend when he was in college, and it never leaves his side when he travels.

"I read it every day and when I'm alone, I pull it out often," he added.

His faith is important to him, and he knows he needs his source of strength to get through each day.

The Big Moment

Do you take your Bible with you on vacation? Or do you forget about reading the Bible when you go away for a few days? You have a lot of things to do on vacations. You might want to build a sandcastle or ride some roller coasters. You may want to spend the day on the beach or hiking a long trail through the woods. These things are all great, but do you leave time to read God's Word?

The Big Play

Now this doesn't mean you carry your Bible to the beach to get sand all over it. But you can keep it in your hotel room or backpack. Jarvis does not take it with him into the huddle and on the football field, but he takes it with him on the airplane or bus. Maybe you can plan a Bible study around a campfire at the end of the day. Don't leave God out of your vacation plans.

The Coach's Corner

God's Word needs to be so important to you that you take it along when you go on a trip. You can also download the app on your phone. But don't leave home without it. All coaches expect their players to know all the plays in the playbook. God hopes you value His playbook enough to read it every day no matter what is on your schedule.

So faith comes from hearing, that is, hearing the Good News about Christ.

—Romans 10:17

CHAPTER 11
YOU ARE UNIQUE

Adam Cimber
MLB Pitcher

You are special.

There is only one of you. You have your own special personality. Your own distinct fingerprint. Your own smile. Your own eyes and ears.

You have your own dreams and your own style. There is something about you that sets you apart from everyone else.

There is no one like Adam Cimber.

His pitching delivery technique is one of a kind.

He copied it from a few pitchers in the past, but he added his own touch.

Adam, who loves chocolate chip pancakes, does not throw to batters in the traditional way like most pitchers. No. That would be too easy and predictable.

When he was younger, he wasn't very big or strong. His dad knew this and came up with an idea for Adam to pitch in a different way. His own way.

When Adam throws to the batter, he uses the submarine style, which has its advantages. The ball is released at a different point and comes into the plate at an unusual angle.

Sometimes batters are thrown off-balance by the distinctive delivery. For Adam, it works.

You should always embrace whom God made you to be. Never try to replicate anyone else.

The Big Moment

Do you have a low opinion of yourself? Maybe someone picks on you or puts you down a lot at school. Maybe you are not the most popular person in class or on your team. Maybe you get left out of conversations and some make fun of you. It's hard to not let that discourage you. But don't ever try to change to be part of the crowd. You are who you are because Jesus made you in His image. Embrace that.

The Big Play

Celebrate you. Find what you are good at and work to develop those skills. Maybe you like to sing or write or play a certain sport. Perhaps you enjoy reading or being with animals. Be happy with who you are because you are one of a kind.

The Coach's Corner

God made you. He designed you, and He has plans He created just for you. This doesn't mean you have to know what your future holds for you right now. Take your time and enjoy being a kid. Laugh and play, but go to church, pray, and read your Bible. Get involved in extracurricular activities and enjoy life. The Lord will let you know His plans for you in time. Don't try to make something happen because it's what you think you want to do. Let Jesus deliver the pitch to you at the right moment. You are so special that God even knows the number of the hairs on your head.

> *"For I know the plans I have for you," says the* LORD. *"They are plans for good and not for disaster, to give you a future and a hope."*
>
> —Jeremiah 29:11

CHAPTER 12
IT WILL BE OKAY

Justin Bethel
NFL Defensive Back

It doesn't matter how old you are, you will experience a setback now and then.

Some problems might be bigger than others, but they are all important to you.

You might have to move and you're afraid to make new friends. Or maybe you didn't make the first string on your ball team. Perhaps you got in trouble at school and anticipate you might also get in trouble when you get home.

Being a kid is not easy.

There might be times when you are too embarrassed to show your face in public. But it will all pass and be okay.

Justin Bethel once faced a problem in football. He had worked his way up to the starting team when he broke his ankle.

In the back of his mind, he did not know if he would ever play football again.

But he wasn't worried because he put his trust in Jesus.

"I had to think that if this turns out to be an injury that keeps me from playing football, then I have to be okay with that," he said. "I had to realize that if that was what God wanted, then He would still take care of me."

His trust in Jesus calmed his spirit. He knew that whatever happened to him, he would be okay as long as he put his faith in the Lord.

How do you handle touchy situations? Do you worry and fret?

The Big Moment

You will be met with some incidents throughout your life that could make you worry. Will you be popular? Where will you go to college if you decide to go? Whom will you marry? What kind of job will you have? Do you want to have children? These are all important questions to ask yourself. But there is no need to be anxious just because you don't have all the answers.

The Big Play

The main thing to remember when you ask yourself these questions is to let God handle all that stuff. This doesn't mean you ignore your schoolwork or never ask anyone out on a date. It means that if you obey God's commandments, read His Word, go to church, and pray, then He has promised to take care of you and help guide you along your journey.

The Coach's Corner

There is a lot going on in your life. Being a kid should be fun and exciting and bring you some of your best memories ever. Your future is ahead of you. That last thing you want to do is bog it down by losing sleep over making major decisions. When you are faced with what to do in a certain situation, talk to your parents or your pastors and ask for their advice. They want what is best for you. But make sure you talk to God first about any choices you need to make.

What's more, I am with you, and I will protect you wherever you go. One day I will bring you back to this land. I will not leave you until I have finished giving you everything I have promised you.

—Genesis 28:15

CHAPTER 13
LET GOD LEAD YOU THROUGH A PROBLEM

Robinson Chirinos
MLB Catcher

Just because you are a kid doesn't mean the devil will leave you alone.

This is not meant to scare you, but Satan will try to influence you and will fight you when you live your life for Jesus.

You must keep your guard up at all times and be on the lookout for his attempts to drag you down and even harm you.

Robinson Chirinos found this out the hard way.

On the same day he accepted Christ as his Savior, he was hit in the head and knocked out during a baseball game. He was catching behind the plate when a foul ball ricocheted off a bat and hit him in the mask. He finished the inning but stumbled back to the dugout. He knew something was wrong.

This was no ordinary concussion.

He became nauseous all the time and vomited a lot. He was dizzy and unable to leave his apartment for weeks because his head hurt.

He did not sleep much and rarely went out.

"I knew I was under attack from the very beginning," he said. "It was a tough time in my life. My whole world was turned upside down. I didn't know if I'd ever play ball again. It was crazy, but I know God brought me through. I could not have made it without Him."

He received treatment from an expert who helped him overcome the bad headaches.

But his faith in God and prayer were the main reasons he was blessed to play baseball the next season.

If the devil gets mad at you, are you brave enough to let Jesus fight your battles?

Satan does not play fair, and he wants you to turn your back on God.

The Big Moment

You might not face physical injury from the devil like Robinson did, but you never know what he will use to attack you. He might make you sick to keep you from attending vacation Bible school or cause a flat tire on your way to Sunday school. He is always looking for ways to throw obstacles in your way if you decide to live for God. Be ready.

The Big Play

Just like you prepare for a game, you have to do things to be ready to face any challenge. Make sure you read your Bible every day, pray every day, and go to church. This will help make you strong and mentally ready to face any problem the devil might throw at you.

The Coach's Corner

You will have problems in life. But always know you can count on Jesus to help you through your troubles. He may not answer right away. Robinson suffered from headaches for a long time before God blessed him to return to his career. The Lord wanted to make sure he was ready. God wants you to be ready too. Always trust Him.

> *The LORD opens the eyes of the blind.*
> *The LORD lifts up those who are weighed down.*
> *The LORD loves the godly.*
>
> —Psalm 146:8

CHAPTER 14

WHAT IS YOUR FAVORITE VERSE?

Derek Carr
NFL Pro Bowl Quarterback

Do you have a favorite verse in the Bible?

It's okay if you don't, but it's something to think about.

A lot of people, especially athletes, have a go-to verse they like to quote to give them inspiration or encouragement.

Sometimes it's helpful to have one when you get nervous, like before a test. Or you may want to whisper some scripture when you get scared, such as right before the roller coaster goes up a big hill.

A short Bible verse that you know by heart can give you assurance when you feel anxious or confused.

Derek Carr has one that he loves.

His favorite verse is, "'For I know the plans I have for you,' says the Lord. 'They are plans for good and not for disaster, to give you a future and a hope'" (Jeremiah 29:11).

He likes this particular scripture so much because his grandfather was a pastor and wanted all his grandchildren to memorize it before he died from cancer.

"He made sure that verse was instilled in us and to know just how good God is to all of us," Derek said. "Even through tough times, he wanted to make sure we knew that, and I love him for that gift."

The verse magnifies the grace God has for His children, and that includes you.

Do you have a verse that is special to you?

The Big Moment

Have you ever been nervous and needed something to calm you down? Some people like to eat when they get nervous while others pace the floor. Worrying is not productive and does not do anyone any good. Have you ever thought of memorizing a verse of scripture to give you peace and comfort?

The Big Play

It won't take long to find a verse in the Bible that you might like enough to memorize. Find one that inspires and makes you feel good and happy. Write it down and repeat it enough to where you won't need to read it anymore because it will be stored away in your brain.

The Coach's Corner

In case you need some suggestions, here are four wonderful verses you might want to learn.

> *For I am with you, and no one will attack and harm you, for many people in this city belong to me.*
>
> —Acts 18:10

> *And I will ask the Father, and he will give you another Advocate, who will never leave you.*
>
> —John 14:16

For I can do everything through Christ, who gives me strength.
                                                            —Philippians 4:13

Trust in the LORD with all your heart;
  do not depend on your own understanding.

                                                            —Proverbs 3:5

These are fantastic verses to learn, but don't limit yourself. The more of God's Word that you know, the stronger you will be and the more you will grow in the Lord.

CHAPTER 15
WHAT IS YOUR THEME SONG?

Corey Dickerson
MLB All-Star Outfielder

The title of this chapter might sound a little weird to you.

A theme song? Who has that? What do they mean? Why have a theme song?

Look at it like this. What song would you want to be associated with you the most?

Just like having a favorite Bible verse, it's cool to have a song that makes your friends think of you—as long as it's not a bad song.

It can be funny or inspirational, and it can also let others know how much you love God.

Corey Dickerson does that when he walks up to the plate when he bats in a Major League Baseball game.

It's called the walk-out song.

He tries to mix it up some, but one season he walked up to the plate with a Jeremy Camp song.

Corey, who loves to watch the movie *The Incredibles* with his kids, says he wants to send the right message to his fans.

"We have a lot of eyes and ears on us when we play ball," he said. "And I want to make sure the songs that are played when I walk up to the plate are appropriate. It's a big way for people to form an opinion about you, and that's important."

Be sure that people hear you listening to music that will have a positive influence on them and help them to have a great impression of you. Be sure to say and do things that will leave them with a good witness of your love for God.

Make sure the songs you listen to send a positive message of hope and encouragement.

The Big Moment

Imagine your Little League or travel team made baseball cards for all the players on your team. The cards would include fun facts about your favorite things such as your favorite movie, dessert, vacation spot, or song. What tune would you list? Would it be a gospel song or one that might raise some eyebrows of concern? Would the song be an inspiration or an embarrassment?

The Big Play

You don't have to listen to Christian music all the time. There are a lot of good songs performed by popular artists in different genres, and that's okay. But if there is any doubt that the song you listen to is appropriate, and it might send a bad message, turn it off.

The Coach's Corner

Your reputation is valuable. You want people to have a good opinion of you, and the things you listen to make up a part of the big picture. Avoid songs that contain bad language or that portray police officers in a bad light. There are millions of songs out there. Find ones that are good and send the message of hope and salvation.

> *Come, let us sing to the LORD!*
> *Let us shout joyfully to the Rock of our salvation.*
> *Let us come to him with thanksgiving.*
> *Let us sing psalms of praise to him.*
>
> —Psalm 95:1–2

CHAPTER 16
DON'T BE EMBARRASSED

C. J. Uzomah
NFL Tight End

Some kids can be cruel and make fun of others. But hopefully you are not one of them.

A number of them like to pick on others because they feel inferior and don't have much self-esteem. Many of these kids bully others.

But hopefully, you are not like that. You should always try to encourage and inspire your family and friends.

It doesn't take much to make a positive difference.

You can open doors for people, post inspirational tweets, and be a positive voice in your community, even at a young age.

Students in your school or on your ball team will take notice and support you. It's easy to sit back and criticize or make fun of others, but it takes someone special to stand up and make a difference.

C. J. Uzomah knows that a lot of people watch what he does, not only on the football field but in life.

He likes to use his social media accounts to let everyone know about his faith.

"I want to send messages of hope and let everyone know I am not afraid to admit that I love Jesus Christ and that

I believe He is my Savior," he said. "I would not be where I am today if it wasn't for God. He has blessed me with ability and talent, and I want to make sure everyone knows that He did it for me."

Are you embarrassed to be called a Christian? Are you scared that others might make fun of you if they find out? Do you hide the fact that you love to go to church?

The Big Moment

When you are with your friends, do you ever mention that you go to church and that you are a follower of Jesus Christ? Do you hesitate to let them know you because they might laugh at you? If that is the case, you need to find some new friends. Ask the Lord to make you bold in your witness for Christ. Jesus died on the cross and rose again on the third day for you. This is amazing, and you should feel pride, gratitude, and honor instead of shame, fear, and anxiety.

The Big Play

You don't have to act like a preacher at school or on the field. But strive to be a light for Jesus and set the standard for others to follow. Show kindness and compassion, but stand firm, and don't back down from your beliefs.

The Coach's Corner

No one wants to be laughed at or made fun of. But when you take a stance and do it with grace and honor, most people will respect your position. If someone makes fun of you, then pray for that person. Never be embarrassed that you serve a living God.

> *For I am not ashamed of this Good News about Christ. It is the power of God at work, saving everyone who believes—the Jew first and also the Gentile.*
>
> —Romans 1:16

CHAPTER 17
FIND A WAY TO WITNESS

Curtis Granderson
MLB All-Star Outfielder

Do you find ways to talk about God to your friends? Does a conversation come naturally with your classmates, or do you have to find ways to let others know you love Jesus?

You don't have to talk about the Lord all the time, but your testimony should be clear.

Kids find many things to talk about with each other—school, movies, trips, friends, ball games, and music. But try to find a way to tell your friends about church, Sunday school, church camp, or Bible school. You get the idea.

Curtis Granderson can relate.

The all-star outfielder, who loves to go to the Waffle House for breakfast, said his faith eventually finds its way into a conversation.

"I went to chapel a few times with a player, but we never spoke about our faith yet," he said. "It just hasn't happened yet. Will we? Mostly likely, but it has to be the right time and the right place."

Make sure you don't force the issue and turn your friends off. If you have a conversation about homework, that might not be the best time to talk about your faith. But God will always give you opportunities to share your testimony, sometimes even by the way you live your life in front of them.

For example, if your friends talk about what they did over the weekend, you could mention that you went to church with your family, or that you attended Sunday school. Take advantage of available opportunities when they present themselves.

The Big Moment

If you are given a chance to tell others that you are a Christian and go to church, do you jump on the opportunity or let it slip away? Are you embarrassed or afraid? Or are you bold and proud that you follow Jesus? Do you tell everyone around you, or do you keep quiet?

The Big Play

There are easy ways to mention church and that you are a Christian that won't upset or offend people. If you play baseball and someone asks you who your favorite player is, you can mention Curtis and say you like him because he's good and he also loves God. Find common ground to talk about and try to squeeze something spiritual into the conversation.

The Coach's Corner

Being popular and liked are important, but you should also want to follow your convictions. If you are part of a conversation where someone is telling a dirty joke, just walk away. Or if a friend is talking bad about someone, try to change the topic or walk away. Or find something good to say about the person they are discussing. Stay positive and be a light to your friends. Show them God's love in everything you do.

> *So, whether you eat or drink, or whatever you do, do it all for the glory of God.*
>
> —1 Corinthians 10:31

CHAPTER 18
IT'S NOT ABOUT YOU

Justin Simmons
NFL All-Pro Defensive Back

You might find this hard to believe, but the world does not revolve around you.

This doesn't mean you are not important, because you are. It means that you should never be selfish.

For instance, if you have a little brother or sister who has a birthday party, don't expect all the attention. Don't blow out the candles and don't unwrap their gifts. You will have your day just like everyone else.

You should never want or demand all the attention from others. The same goes for your friends and ball teams.

If another player has a great game, congratulate him and be genuinely happy for his success. Don't get jealous and try to hog the recognition.

Justin Simmons tries to take this attitude when he plays in the NFL.

To be a good player, there are moments when you have to make the big play and deliver for your team. He tries to separate the two and stay humble.

"There are times when playing football is about being selfish, but you do it for a selfless reason. You make sacrifices for the team," he said. "That's what makes faith different. It's the complete opposite. You do for others without the expectation of being rewarded, except from God when you go to heaven."

If you make a touchdown, then you might expect to be congratulated. But don't forget the other players on your team who helped you make it to the end zone. Give everyone their due credit.

The Big Moment

Do you do things for the right reason—to help others and not to receive fanfare? Have you ever volunteered your time to help people who don't have as much as you? Can you find some clothes you don't wear and donate them to the Salvation Army? Have you thought of getting a few friends together and helping a widow with her lawn care? These are ways to put others first.

The Big Play

Recognition is fun. It's awesome to see your name recognized for making the big play to help win the game or to be honored for awards and recognition you have earned. But don't let it go to your head and give you a big ego. "Faith is about serving others and loving on others and helping others," Justin said. "It can be hard to stay disciplined at times in the league, but I have to make myself because it's the right thing."

The Coach's Corner

Humility is a wonderful characteristic to have. When you are humble and thankful, you will want to put the needs of others in front of yours. Be happy for your classmates and teammates who do well. Lift them up and encourage them. Your turn will come.

> *And he gives grace generously. As the Scriptures say, "God opposes the proud but gives grace to the humble."*
>
> —James 4:6

CHAPTER 19
SHINE FOR JESUS

Tim Tebow
MLB Outfielder

When you live for God, He gives you lots of reasons to smile.

He forgives all your sins. He is preparing a place for you to live with Him in heaven. He is a close friend and someone you can depend on.

That is enough right there to make you smile.

But there are also some things you can do for others to make them feel important.

Tim Tebow does his best to let his light shine for some special people.

He is the head of the Tim Tebow Foundation, which hosts a large event each year called "The Night to Shine Prom."

At this event, thousands of people from all over the world come together for one evening to make sure people with special needs have a night dedicated just to them.

When Tim was fifteen, he was on a mission trip overseas and met a boy who was born with his feet backwards. Some people thought the boy had a curse, but not Tim. He hugged him and showed him God's love. The passion to help others came alive that day. The foundation was soon started, and the Night to Shine was born.

The event is huge and takes place all over the world. People with special needs get dressed up and attend a prom. Thousands of people volunteer to make sure the night is one of a kind.

"It's such a part of our identity and our worth about understanding how much God loves us," Tim said. "For us to be able to help this community to where the biggest event in their city and their town is for them to understand their worth. It's not enough that they know that we love them, but the God of this universe loves them."

The Night to Shine puts smiles on everyone's faces.

The Big Moment

Can you think of something you can do to make someone smile and feel special? Maybe you know a friend who has been sad or even sick and needs a reason to laugh. Perhaps a new kid just moved into your neighborhood or joined your team, and you can tell he is nervous. You can take action to reach out and make them smile.

The Big Play

Being nice and being a friend are not hard. All you have to do is start a conversation with a smile. Offer to sit with them or introduce them to your friends. Also make a point to invite them to church or Sunday school.

The Coach's Corner

As a child of God, you are called to be an example and a lighthouse to those who are lost or in the dark. You should be friendly and strive to make them feel important. Never think of yourself as better than anyone else, and go out of your way to help someone in need. Make someone feel special today.

> *And the very hairs on your head are all numbered. So don't be afraid; you are more valuable to God than a whole flock of sparrows.*
>
> —Luke 12:7

CHAPTER 20
IT WILL ALL BE OKAY

Tyrod Taylor
NFL Pro Bowl Quarterback

As a kid growing up, you will face some tough choices.

You will also see your fair share of problems. No one likes to think about it, but difficult times will come to all.

That's why it's important to surround yourself with a solid base of friends and family to help you through those moments.

When your faith is under fire, this is when you lean on God and your supporters the most.

The best thing about Jesus is that He wants to know everything about you. Sometimes, although it's not intentional, some friends might not be too interested in your stories. Everyone is busy and consumed with their own lives.

Tyrod Taylor is aware of this too. He's had his share of problems, but he always falls back on his faith.

"I've definitely come across a few challenges along the way," he said. "But everything goes back to faith and that foundation that is so important."

Tyrod, who loves French toast for breakfast, was benched as the starting quarterback when he thought he should have kept his job. He was upset and let the Lord know.

"That's just how it goes sometimes," he said. "Without my faith, I think I would have folded in that situation because it was hard. I think God puts you in those situations and allows things to happen to see how you respond."

How would you act? What if you lost out on getting a part in the school play when you really thought you would get it? Perhaps you were benched on the ball team or failed geometry class.

The Big Moment

You will face adversity in your life. No one likes to be put through trying times, but they will happen. Try not to be bitter and cry out that life is not fair. You might have to move away from your friends because your parents have to relocate for a job. Or maybe you did something to warrant being placed in detention. Perhaps a loved one is sick, and you feel helpless.

The Big Play

The best thing to do under these conditions is to go to God in prayer, read your Bible, and talk to a spiritual mentor. Sometimes you don't have to understand what has happened, but you have to accept it and move on. Find a way to come back when it seems like you're losing the game.

The Coach's Corner

In times like these, Jesus will be your best friend and place of comfort and rest. You can find a quiet place and ask Him for guidance and pour out your heart to Him. You will later look back and see how He took care of you. He may not answer your prayer how you wanted, but His way is always best.

Don't worry about anything; instead, pray about everything.
Tell God what you need, and thank him for all he has done.
                                                        —Philippians 4:6

CHAPTER 21
LET GOD CHANGE YOUR LIFE

Dave Jauss
MLB Coach

Big league coaches like Dave Jauss see the good and bad in baseball. Dave has been part of winning teams and others that didn't do so good.

He loves being around the game and spending time on the diamond playing field.

Dave loves his life and how God has taken care of him and his family through the years.

He grew up in church and was taught right from wrong at an early age. He lived a good life and treated everyone with love and compassion. Dave was doing everything right, or so he thought.

Then one day he realized that being a Christian is more than just going through the motions. He actively attended church, stayed involved, and prayed. But he knew something was missing.

One day he realized his life could be fulfilled by surrendering everything to the Lord.

"When I found out that Jesus wanted a personal relationship with me, it all changed," he said. "I was able to release the control of my life and give it to Him."

Once he did, Dave appreciated life even more.

"My outlook changed, and I looked at what I could do to serve Him, and not what He could do for me," he said. "Once I did that, my life seemed to fall into place."

Dave tries his best to be a good role model and to point players to God if they ask about his faith. "I don't shove it on anyone, but they can watch me and my life and if they have any questions, they know they can always ask me. Because I love to tell my story and how God changed my life."

Do you have a personal relationship with Jesus? Being a good person and helping others is great. But it's all in vain if you don't know Jesus as your personal savior.

Are there times you check all the boxes but feel like something is missing?

The Big Moment

Dave didn't realize that he could have a personal relationship with God until he was an adult. He went to church, but he didn't have that special relationship Jesus offers. Do you have one?

The Big Play

You can also have a deeper relationship with Christ by acknowledging that Jesus was crucified, rose from the grave, and is preparing a mansion for you in heaven. Do your best to put Him first in your life, and let the Holy Spirit lead you.

The Coach's Corner

Being a kid is busy enough. There is so much going on in your life that every day seems like a blur. But be sure to make time for God. He made the universe for you.

> *But when you pray, go away by yourself, shut the door behind you, and pray to your Father in private. Then your Father, who sees everything, will reward you.*
> —Matthew 6:6

CHAPTER 22
BE THANKFUL IN ALL SITUATIONS

Mark Ingram
NFL Running Back

Do you thank God for all the accomplishments you have in life so far? Do you also thank God for your problems? This might sound crazy, but maybe you should. Sometimes overcoming challenges can lead to great victories.

Most teenagers have not achieved great accomplishments yet. Your biggest successes at this point in your life might be making a ball team or getting straight A's on your report card. This is a big deal, and you should never take these things for granted.

The same goes for special moments in our personal lives. Always cherish time spent with family, and consider each day of life a blessing.

Be thankful for good health. Be grateful for the unique things in your life that give you your own distinct personality and circumstances. Appreciate the challenges you face as God allows problems to happen in your life to shape your character and to make you a stronger person.

Mark Ingram has this positive attitude.

"I know everything I have been able to accomplish in my life comes from the Lord," he said. "The walk with Christ is not perfect, you know, no Christian is perfect. We all can work to strive to be better and be more like Him each and every day. But I am thankful the Lord has given me this opportunity."

Even when Mark, who said his wife makes the best and craziest breakfast casseroles, got in a little trouble with the NFL and had to sit out a few games, he knew God had a plan.

"That was a tough time," he said. "But that's when I relied on my faith and looked at what the Lord was trying to tell me though all that."

Mark knows he is blessed and thanks Jesus every day for His kindness.

The Big Moment

Are there times when you might not feel blessed? Perhaps you got into trouble at school or faced some disciplinary actions from authorities. Your instinct is to hide the truth and to be afraid. But it's also a time to learn.

The Big Play

The best thing to do when things go wrong is to own up to your mistakes and accept the consequences. The more you hide from the truth, the worse the situation will become. In the end, God can make you better and stronger. Things might get ugly for a time, but if you accept accountability for your actions and work to make things right, God can bless your story and work it all out for the best. Sometimes, life lessons are tough but beneficial.

The Coach's Corner

Don't dwell in the past but make a point to learn from your mistakes. When you realize you have made a bad turn, quickly assume responsibility and move forward before it's too late. Be thankful for all situations, and use them as learning experiences. God is good, and you can trust Him to take care of you and point you in the right direction. Seek the Lord for forgiveness and ask for His guidance. He will always be there to provide it for you.

For we are each responsible for our own conduct.
—Galatians 6:5

CHAPTER 23
LINE YOURSELF UP RIGHT

Clint Hurdle
MLB Manager

Have you ever had good intentions to do something right, but things all went haywire?

Maybe you studied hard for an important test but didn't pass.

Or perhaps you worked long hours perfecting your swing at home and at practice, only to strike out four times in the next game.

You will have days like that. You just have to keep working and preparing.

Clint Hurdle compares life in general to the game of golf.

"You might be able to hit the ball 400 yards, but it doesn't matter if you are not lined up correctly," he said. "The ball will go in the wrong direction and out of bounds."

When Clint played in the MLB, he had a lot of potential, but he didn't live up to expectations. He was not very nice to people and found himself alone at times.

This is when he realized he needed to get his life lined up in the right direction.

"Life has been amazing once I realized it was going the wrong way," he said. "I am aligned now with Christ, and my life needs to be that of a servant."

He describes his life as a Christian obstacle course. He has seen the ups and downs of professional baseball and life too. He's coached in the World Series, and he has also been fired from ball teams. He's learned the hard way that you cannot make everyone happy. But he tries to encourage and inspire with the Word of God.

"It had not been a walk in the park," he said. "But I'm thankful God sees fit to guide me now because I surrendered my life over to Him."

Are there things in your life you need to turn over to God?

The Big Moment

If you are doing something you have to hide from your parents, friends, or teachers, then you should not be doing it in the first place. Maybe you are being pressured at school to try a cigarette, drugs, or alcohol. The temptation to give in to peer pressure is real, so you must trust God to keep you lined up in the right direction so you will have the power to say no.

The Big Play

The devil will try to trick you into doing things you know you will regret. He tries to entice you by making them look harmless and fun. But there is no enjoyment in disappointing or hurting the people who are closest to you. When temptation comes your way, step back and look at the target. In this case, your ultimate goal is to please Jesus and go to heaven someday. Line yourself up in the right direction and smash the golf ball 400 yards.

The Coach's Corner

Temptation is real, and you face it every day. Once you realize you cannot fight Satan off by yourself, call on the Lord to make you stronger and give you the ability to resist. You must realize you are no match for the devil alone. You need God to be your leadoff hitter as well as your base runner and cleanup hitter. Cheer Him on around the bases as He scores the winning run.

> *So humble yourselves before God. Resist the devil, and he will flee from you.*
>
> —James 4:7

CHAPTER 24
FIND YOUR PASSION

Mike Tomlin
NFL Head Coach

Anyone who knows Mike Tomlin is aware of his passion for life. His players love him because he is so excited about football and loves to coach.

He lets his positive energy show everywhere he goes. And he does more than just talk.

Coach Mike puts actions to his words and backs up why he believes the way he does.

He is involved with an organization that helps find and rescue young kids who have been kidnapped by bad people.

Sadly, this kind of thing does happen, and you need to always be on the lookout and always be cautious of strangers.

But Coach Mike does more than just talk about it. He does something about it.

"I cannot find a man who could stand against this," he said. "There are a lot of different interests of things that are important for them to fight for and I get it. But anyone who can't get behind this cause . . . I don't know about them."

Coach Mike donates his time and money to help this cause, which he believes in from the bottom of his heart. He has a mission and wants to help in every way he can.

He considers it a mission field to help children.

What about you? Is there a cause or a charity that you have helped out? There are many clubs and organizations you can join even as a young person.

But first, you must have a passion and desire to help others.

The Big Moment

Your first step is to realize you can make an impact on the lives of those around you. You don't have to get involved with a huge organization or a cause that supports worldwide. You can make a difference in your own town or city.

The Big Play

Ask your parents, friends, or teachers about ways you can help. You can offer to cut the grass of an elderly widow in your community. You can pick up trash in your neighborhood or take care of a lost pet and try to find the owner. While it is a lot of fun to play video games or hang out with friends, God also expects you to set aside some time to help others.

The Coach's Corner

When you put time in your schedule to try to make a positive impact on those around you, then you are doing what

Jesus wants you to do. He wants you to be an ambassador for Him by spreading the good news of the gospel and reaching out to help.

> *You are the light of the world—like a city on a hilltop that cannot be hidden. No one lights a lamp and then puts it under a basket. Instead, a lamp is placed on a stand, where it gives light to everyone in the house. In the same way, let your good deeds shine out for all to see, so that everyone will praise your heavenly Father.*
>
> —Matthew 5:14–16

CHAPTER 25
DON'T BE AFRAID TO DREAM

Albert Pujols
MLB All-Star First Baseman, MVP

Have you ever heard that you can be anything you want to be? Does anyone tell you to dream big and go after your goals?

This all sounds great, and you should chase your dreams, because otherwise, you won't find them. No one is going to pursue them for you.

You won't make it to home plate if you don't swing the bat to get a hit to reach first base.

There is a lot of work and planning that goes into reaching your potential.

Albert Pujols knows about chasing dreams. Nicknamed "The Machine," he was not drafted until the thirteenth round in 1999 by the St. Louis Cardinals. Can you believe there were some teams who did not think he was a good player?

But Albert believed in himself, and he knew God was going to take care of him.

"Sometimes you might hear that you'll never be able to accomplish something you want," Albert said. "In God's eyes, we will be anything He wants us to be. We just have to accept the plan."

Are you willing to do what Jesus wants you to do? What if

you want to play baseball, but the Lord has other ideas for your life? Will you trust Him?

Be open and willing to follow God's plan. Who knows? His strategy might lead you to your dream job.

"Growing up, I never really expected to be where I am today, but God gets all the glory," he said. "It just goes to show that you have to let the Lord develop you into what He wants."

The Big Moment

Never be afraid to have a big dream. It will give you incentive and motivation to prepare yourself for a successful future. But when things don't go the way you planned, then you adjust but always have a goal. If you want to play professional baseball, you will have to put in hours of work and dedication, listen to your coaches and mentors, and seek God's guidance.

The Big Play

Life is full of success and some failure along the way. If you reach your destination, then praise God for his blessings. If Jesus wants you to go in another direction, then thank Him for keeping you from something He did not think was best for you. Never take failure personally, but rather see it as a signal from the Lord to go another way to a new beginning.

The Coach's Corner

Never give up on your dreams. They might come true when you are in high school, in college, or even many years later.

But God's timing is always right, so be sure to listen to what God tells you to do and never rush His plan. The key to unlocking your dreams is to praise the Lord for His blessings ahead of time. That way you will never strike out.

Praise the Lord!
Praise God in his sanctuary;
  praise him in his mighty heaven!

—Psalm 150:1

CHAPTER 26
GOD HAS BIGGER PLANS FOR YOU

Tim Tebow
NFL Quarterback

Have you thought about what you want to do when you grow up?

Maybe you want to play football or own your own business. Perhaps you want to be a teacher or a coach. No matter what you want, always trust God's plan for your life.

Also keep in mind that while your plans don't always work out the way you might want them to, pray that they will always work out for His glory.

Just ask Tim Tebow.

He won a national championship in college football two times with the University of Florida and was recognized with the Heisman Trophy for being the best player in the nation, among other awards. The Denver Broncos drafted him in 2010.

Although he won ball games, he was traded to the New York Jets, who eventually cut him. It seemed that he just could not find a home to play football.

So, he returned to his first love of baseball and went to play for the New York Mets' minor league system for a couple seasons. In spite of his talent, they also let him go.

But he's not discouraged. He knows Jesus will provide for Him.

"That's the great thing about God," Tim said. "No matter what, He will always be my rock and support system. I know He will take care of me."

God might have closed the doors for him to continue his career as a professional athlete so He could open up new and exciting opportunities for Tim's future.

What you think you want could actually be far from what the Lord has in store for you. God might let you tinker with what you want to do, but He will eventually show you a roadmap that may lead to even bigger and better plans for your life.

The Big Moment

You might be an outstanding football player in junior high or high school and think the NFL is in your future. It might be. But be prepared for the Lord to show you another avenue. Never be too stubborn to accept God's plan for your life.

The Big Play

Instead of constantly thinking about scholarship offers from college football coaches or visits from professional scouts, try to focus on your grades and be a standout academic student in case sports does not work out. This will give you a backup plan to attract potential employers. Treat your family and true friends with respect because they will stick by you no matter what happens.

The Coach's Corner

To have a dream and want to reach a goal is important. But how you handle disappointment is also critical. When God shuts a door, accept it and thank Him for taking care of you. He always sees the big picture for your life. Praise Him and be excited for what He has in store for you next.

But blessed are those who trust in the LORD
and have made the LORD their hope and confidence.
                                        —Jeremiah 17:7

CHAPTER 27
MAKE THE STATEMENT

Daniel Stumpf
MLB Pitcher

Do you put anything on your sports equipment as a witness to others that you are a child of God?

Some players, like Albert Pujols, put scripture on their cleats, and others have their favorite verses burned into a bat.

And many of them, like Daniel Stumpf, have the Word of God engraved on their baseball gloves. Daniel has the name of his son and Psalm 98:12 written on his baseball glove.

When people or fans see his glove, they know that he loves his child and Jesus too.

For him, it's the best way to tell everyone what is important in his life.

"That way they know that God, my faith, and my son are the biggest parts of my life," he said. "It's always good to look down at my glove and see that."

With a lot of eyes on him when he is on the pitcher's mound, he wants to make sure everyone knows he is a Christian and a father.

"It's a good way to send the message out," he said. "Kids like to look at gloves, and I like it when they see mine because they see the Word of God on mine."

Daniel is not ashamed to tell anyone who sees his gear that he is a Christian.

Would you want your parents or pastor to see what is written on your wristbands, batting gloves, or on the visor of your hat?

Would you be proud or ashamed?

The Big Moment

You don't have to put Christian symbols or words on your sports gear, but it's not a bad idea either. It's the perfect way to witness to your friends and be a good role model. It can be a good conversation piece too if someone wants to know about your faith.

The Big Play

Once you decide to post some scripture for others to see, find one that has a special meaning for you personally. Find one that inspires or sends a message. Remember when Tim Tebow used to put scripture on his eye black? When he played in the 2009 national championship game and displayed John 3:16 under his eyes, 94 million people googled the scripture online and hopefully read about the plan of salvation.

The Coach's Corner

Consider making a statement of faith for your teammates to see. Some may laugh, but be sure to stand strong and defend God's Word. Keep in mind that after you proclaim

God's truth, the pressure is on for you to live it. Make the statement and be bold. Don't back down and give in to peer pressure. Make others curious so they will ask you why you are so happy and what God means to you.

Let the fields and their crops burst out with joy!
Let the trees of the forest sing for joy.

—Psalm 96:12

CHAPTER 28
GOD IS ALWAYS GOOD

Minkah Fitzpatrick
NFL Defensive Back

When something bad happens, do you still think God is good?

Maybe someone close to you became sick and went through a long recovery. Or perhaps something you loved was stolen, or maybe you were injured in a car accident.

Do these circumstances affect your relationship with Jesus?

Minkah Fitzpatrick went through a difficult time.

When he was in high school, a terrible storm hit, and he and his family lost their home and everything they owned.

The family had nowhere to stay and had to move into a basement with relatives for an entire year.

This situation must have been difficult. You don't realize what all you take for granted sometimes until it's gone. His family may have had to share a basement, but it could have been worse. Fortunately, no one was killed when their house was destroyed.

Minkah knew the Lord would take care of him and his family, and He did. God still made a way for Minkah to play college football at Alabama and then go on to the NFL.

"My faith is the main reason I play this game," he said. "My faith and belief in God allows me to go through the ups and downs of life. No matter what I go through, I know He will be consistent. Through all of everything we went through, He was always there, and He got us through our struggles."

Because he and his family were faithful to the Lord during a bad time, Minkah said he is now reaping the benefits of God's promises. He does not consider himself lucky—but blessed.

"We just always gave God glory and credit through it all," he added.

Minkah never lost faith, and neither should you.

The Big Moment

Bad things will happen to you during your life. You might go through something traumatic such as what Minkah and his family faced, but hopefully you won't. But no matter what mountains you face, always keep your faith strong.

The Big Play

When difficult times come your way, it's easy to try to solve problems yourself. But instead, use these situations as opportunities to improve your prayer life and spend more time reading the Word of God. This will boost your relationship with God and give you peace during the storm.

The Coach's Corner

Faith gets stronger the more you use it and apply it to your life. It's easy to praise God when life is good. But when you face a trial, call on Jesus. He wants you to know that He loves you and He will take care of you. You just need to trust Him.

Surely your goodness and unfailing love will pursue me
  all the days of my life,
and I will live in the house of the LORD
  forever.

—Psalm 23:6

CHAPTER 29
WORK HARD FOR GOD

Clayton Kershaw
MLB Cy Young Award-Winning Pitcher

You are not too young to work for the Lord. Much of your time might be taken up with schoolwork and extracurricular activities. You may also have baseball or band practice to attend, or maybe you are a cheerleader or member of quiz bowl.

And of course, there is social time with friends.

Busy people often get things done. They know how to prioritize what matters most.

Clayton Kershaw is an example of someone who is good at this.

He loves to work hard and practice baseball, and his accomplishments prove this.

The multiple-award-winning pitcher is known to stay on schedule with his workout routines because he does not want to let his teammates down.

When he's not crunching cookies or watching his favorite movie, *Dumb and Dumber,* he's either practicing his job or working for the Lord.

He and his wife founded and operate a nonprofit organization to help underprivileged kids who are sick get the medicine they need. They also share the gospel of Jesus.

"If you work for the Lord, great things will happen," he said. "I work hard every day at this game, and I also want to work hard for the Lord. This helps me to remember what God did for me and puts things into proper perspective. "

Try to carve time out of your schedule to do something productive for God. It might be a sacrifice but think about what He gave for you when He sent His son to die on the cross for your sins.

"Life is a grind just like baseball," Clayton said. "You have to work hard at it and then get up the next day and work hard at it again."

The Big Moment

If you don't have time to do something positive for God, then you are too busy. Something needs to go. You must realize that Jesus died for you so you could live in heaven if you choose to follow Him. Surely you can give a few minutes each week for the cause of Christ.

The Big Play

There are a lot of activities you can do to be a witness for the Lord. You can donate your time at a food bank once a week or volunteer to work at Bible School or Junior Church. Talk to your parents or pastors about getting more involved in youth groups and becoming an active disciple for God. Organize a prayer group at school or start a Bible Club.

The Coach's Corner

You can make time for God if you want to. Talk it over with some Christian friends and do something positive. But once you start, make the commitment and stick with it. A coach doesn't like it if you only show up on game days, and the Lord will notice if you slack off on your spiritual commitments as well. Work hard in all you do, especially in what you do for the Kingdom.

> *Work willingly at whatever you do, as though you were working for the Lord rather than for people.*
> —Colossians 3:23

CHAPTER 30
WHO ARE YOU IN GOD'S EYES?

Benjamin Watson
NFL Super Bowl-Winning Tight End

Do you know who you are? Are you a good student? Are you the star player of your team?

Perhaps you struggle with your identity. You want to do great things, but circumstances hold you back. You have a desire to stand out, but you feel like you have blended into the crowd just to become another number.

Or maybe you have devoted yourself to one thing in life, when God suddenly wakes you up and shows you that He has something else planned for you.

Benjamin Watson knows that feeling.

For the first part of his career in the NFL, he devoted most of his time to his craft. He wanted to be the best.

He was injured his first year and spent many hours trying to make a comeback.

His entire life was football. It consumed him.

"There were times when my identity was wrapped up in football. It's all I was," he said. "I worked out, watched film, and studied all the time. Football was my whole life."

Eventually, God got his attention and made him aware that there were more important things in life. Benjamin was a football player, but that's not all Jesus wanted him to be.

"God gives us different talents, and we should always give our all to those things. But I was taking what was going on in my physical journey with football and transferring it over to my spiritual walk," he said. "And that is not where we need to be."

The Lord opened doors for Benjamin to start speaking out and getting involved with issues of concern to him. He wrote a book and began to discuss pro-life issues, and today he is in high demand to share his spiritual wisdom around the country.

This is whom God wanted Benjamin to be.

Who are you?

The Big Moment

There may be more to life for you than being an honor student or catching touchdown passes. God may ask you to use your platform to share the good news of Jesus in your school and your community. You can make a difference.

The Big Play

You should be involved in extracurricular activities because those are important in personal development. But so are charitable organization. So is taking a leadership role, like student government, in your school. What is God asking you to do?

The Coach's Corner

If you feel you need to be a more active witness, kick your prayer life up a notch, and dive into the Word of God more often. Avoid making hasty decisions, and don't make any commitments without seeking His will first. Don't be afraid to trust God when He wants you to do something. Be whom the Lord directs you to be.

My old self has been crucified with Christ. It is no longer I who live, but Christ lives in me. So I live in this earthly body by trusting in the Son of God, who loved me and gave himself for me.

—Galatians 2:20

CHAPTER 31
OVERCOME YOUR CHALLENGES

Brian Dozier
MLB All-Star Second Baseman

Have you ever wondered why something bad happened?

Maybe you didn't get the lead part in the school play, or you struck out with the bases loaded. Perhaps you were excited to begin the season at shortstop, but an injury kept you off the field for the entire season.

How would you deal with one of these situations?

Brian Dozier went through a similar ordeal.

He had the opportunity to skip his senior year of college and enter the MLB draft, but he decided to stay with his team and wait another year to turn pro. This was a major decision, since he was a surefire bet to the make it into the Big Leagues.

But then he smashed his shoulder and had to have several pins put in it to heal.

He was discouraged because he thought he threw away his chances to play professional baseball.

Why did this happen? What good would come out of it?

"I didn't know it at the time, but what I went through was a true blessing in disguise," Brian said. "The Lord knew what He was doing, but I didn't at the time."

Brian used that year to learn how to become a leader. He helped others and encouraged his teammates.

Instead of leading his team on the field, he had to do it from the dugout.

And players responded. They looked up to Brian because he stayed with his team and supported them.

"That time I was hurt was a wonderful growing experience for me," he said. "I don't know if I'd be the leader I am today had it not been for that."

And by the way, Brian went on to enjoy an all-star-studded career in baseball.

The Big Moment

You are ready for the big move and your time to shine, but your plans don't work out. How do you respond? Do you get upset and pout, or do you look at it as an opportunity to grow, like Brian did? Do you pray and ask God how to help you find something positive in your circumstances, or do you become frustrated and want to quit?

The Big Play

Ask Jesus to teach you and show you how to rebound from tough situations. You don't have to understand why God allows bad things to happen to you, but trust that He will bring you through. It's okay to ask questions, but be disciplined and follow His game plan.

The Coach's Corner

As a result of Brian's injury, he developed leadership skills that later carried him into his professional career. When it first happened, he was discouraged, but eventually he understood why God allowed him to experience his injury. God took a difficult situation and helped him to grow in the middle of his struggle. The Lord provided a way for him to overcome his challenges, and in the long run, Brian was a better person and a better player. Be open to accepting God's plan for you.

For you have rescued me from my troubles
and helped me to triumph over my enemies.

—Psalm 54:7

CHAPTER 32
SHOW DEDICATION

Andy Dalton
NFL All-Pro Quarterback

There is a lot of pressure on kids in sports today. Some move from one team to another in hopes of winning a championship.

Young athletes watch professionals do this. At the college level, players often come into a program and leave after one year to chase their dreams in the pros and make a lot of money.

And this trend is now influencing high school and even younger athletes.

Travel teams are good, but there is still something to be said for dedication to a team.

It's also important to be dedicated to God and your family.

Andy Dalton is committed to his profession, his Lord, and his wife. And he wants everyone to know that.

To reinforce his allegiance, he works hard to be the best quarterback he can, attends Bible studies, and wears his wedding band at all times. In his case, he wears a rubber Qalo ring.

"I am married, and to wear a ring and not have to worry about it getting damaged is nice," he said. "I want everyone to know I'm married, and I have no reason to take this ring off."

When you make a commitment, be bold enough to follow through.

That is a sign of integrity and honor.

If you are on a team that is not doing well, it's easy to consider transferring to a different school district to play for a better program.

A lot of kids do this because they want to win and have an opportunity to go to the next level. That is a decision you might face someday, but it should be discussed with your family, and you should also pray about it.

Don't just leave because the going gets tough. You may want to stick around and show what you are made of. The same is true for your relationship with Jesus.

When life gets difficult, don't jump teams and move over to the other side. Remember that without God on your team, you will always lose.

Be dedicated.

The Big Moment

You are not having the best season. You have thrown a few interceptions and your team is 2-5. Another coach has talked to you about moving to his district to play, but your friends and family want you to stay and finish your obligation. What will you do?

The Big Play

Don't abandon your team when the chips are down. In the face of adversity, reach down and find the will to win. The same is true in your spiritual walk with God. You might face an obstacle that weakens your faith. The devil whispers to you that you will have more success on his team. But you know that is a lie. Rebuke him and get back in the huddle with your team to fight the good fight.

The Coach's Corner

Sometimes it might be tempting to choose a different direction, but it may not be what's best for you or for those around you. Dedication and commitment are sometimes more important than the final outcome. Andy knows how important it is to let everyone know he is dedicated to his team on the field, and to his wife and God all the time. Live up to your obligations and be faithful to the team you choose.

Never let loyalty and kindness leave you!

Tie them around your neck as a reminder.
  Write them deep within your heart.

—Proverbs 3:3

CHAPTER 33
YOU CAN'T GET AWAY FROM GOD

Michael Lorenzen
MLB Pitcher

Have you ever made fun of someone? Perhaps later you felt bad and realized you shouldn't have done it.

But when Michael's friends did it, he couldn't sleep.

When he was a junior in high school, he was the real deal. He knew he was going to turn into a major league pitcher. But he was also a bit of a rebel.

Without any real role models or any church influence in his life, he later tried drugs and alcohol.

One homecoming school night, he and some friends were at Huntington Beach Pier when they heard an older man talking and spouting off to people. They were curious about what he was saying because they had never seen him before.

The man was preaching the Gospel of Jesus Christ. He told Michael and his friends that God loved them and could forgive them of their sins. His friends made fun of the preacher and laughed at him.

Although Michael admitted he was high on drugs at the time, he couldn't get the story out of his mind about the man who died for his sins. He heard the words over and over again all through the night.

"I got convicted right there," he said. "I was high, but I knew right from wrong. I knew what I was doing was wrong, and I needed to change my life."

He tried to sleep, but the words about the Savior stayed with him. "Until then, I'd had a false sense about God," Michael said.

A few days later, he and his brother attended Calvary Chapel of Costa Mesa. Michael was miserable and knew what to do. He asked God to save him and turned his life around.

"I don't know who that man was, but he told me the truth," he said. "He had the courage to tell me and my friends about Jesus. I'll always admire that man."

The Big Moment

Have you heard the Gospel of Christ presented to you? How did it make you feel? Did you laugh it off? Have you ever made fun of a classmate because they go to church? Or maybe you have been on the receiving end. Perhaps you tried to invite friends to church or a youth outing and they laughed at you. Do you feel embarrassed and give up, or do you keep inviting them?

The Big Play

If someone makes fun of you, don't let it discourage you. Stay strong and stick to your beliefs. Michael's friends laughed at the preacher, but that didn't stop him from telling the truth. Because of him, one person at the right time heard words of encouragement that changed his life. Don't ever ridicule someone for trying to be a light in a dark world.

The Coach's Corner

It takes guts to tell someone about the saving grace of God. Ask the Lord to give you the determination and power that you need to be a witness for Christ. Michael's whole future changed because of what the preacher said on the pier that night. Will you be bold and tell the good news of the gospel to others?

> *And then he told them, "Go into all the world and preach the Good News to everyone."*
>
> —Mark 16:15

CHAPTER 34
BE THE EXAMPLE

Ben Roethlisberger
NFL Quarterback

Whom do you admire? Is there someone you want to be like when you grow up?

Be careful about setting people up on pedestals because sometimes they can let you down. After all, they are human beings just like you.

Sometimes, people you might look up to will make mistakes. Big ones. No one is perfect. But even more important is the way they respond to their blunders.

If someone is sorry and makes the effort to learn from their faults, this is better than continuing to do the wrong thing without any remorse whatsoever.

Most fathers want their kids to be successful as an adult. But how do they define success? Money? A big house? Does it matter what you own?

As a kid, you probably want a good role model to look up to. You want someone who genuinely cares about you and not about how much money you have.

That is the kind of dad Ben had as a child.

"I hope and pray that I can have half the relationship with my kids that I had with my dad growing up," Ben Roethlisberger said. "With my children, they make me strive to be the best father and husband I can be. I have a huge responsibility, and I can't let them down."

Kids want a godly father they can depend on when problems arise. They want someone who cares enough about them to say no and protect them from harm and bad choices.

Ben's dad took him to church and made sure the future All-Pro had a solid understanding of the Lord.

"He is a godly man, an amazing father and husband. So I strive to be half the man he is, because there is no way I can be like him," he added. "He is as good as they come."

It's not too early to start thinking about what kind of a parent you want to be someday. Even though this is a long time away, you are molding and shaping your character while you are still young.

The Big Moment

Do you set the example for others to follow? As a teammate, do your fellow players see you pray at lunch? Do they know you go to church and attend youth group activities? What kind of reputation do you have? Do others see you as an honest and trusting person, or are you a goof-off who takes God's blessings for granted?

The Big Play

You are never too young to start planning for the future. Set the tone now to be a child of God and one whom others look up to and depend on. Once they know you care about

them, you are accountable to live a Christian life in front
of them, and this will help you become a stronger leader.

The Coach's Corner

As a spiritual leader, here are some important steps to follow. Arrange to bring together a Bible study or a prayer
group before or after practice once a week or at least each
month. Don't be discouraged if only a few people show up.
Stay with it and be dedicated. Or find another way to share
the message of God's love. The point is to be a light to others to spread the good news of Jesus Christ.

> *Without wise leadership, a nation falls;*
> *there is safety in having many advisers.*
>
> —Proverbs 11:14

CHAPTER 35
DON'T GO THROUGH THE MOTIONS

Adam Wainwright
MLB Pitcher

When Adam was seven years old, he wanted to be like his older brother.

In his eyes, his brother did everything right, and he looked up to him in every way.

His brother was valedictorian of his class and an Eagle Scout. They did everything together, including going to church.

But at the time, Adam was not a Christian, but his brother lived by faith.

"I was doing things okay," Adam said. "I wasn't a bad person. I was cool, I thought."

But deep down, he knew he wasn't right with God.

The years passed, and he got the opportunity to attend a Professional Athletes Outreach meeting where he was told about how a Christian relationship is supposed to be—a real connection with God.

Most of his life, he had followed the example his brother set. But he had never experienced his own real relationship with the Lord.

He went through the motions and played church for years, but he had doubts about if salvation was real.

But after the encounter with PAO, something changed.

He understood how his life could be so much better if he had his own personal relationship with Jesus instead of pretending to have one.

It wasn't about what the Lord could do for Adam, but instead about what He had already done for him.

Adam also discovered that he could find true salvation that was real. When he embraced the truth and accepted Christ, his life suddenly had meaning and a purpose.

Now Adam no longer needed a role model to follow, because he found all he needed was to trust and believe in Christ.

The Big Moment

Do you go through the motions and play church? Do you have questions like Adam did about whether the Christian walk is real? Maybe a certain prayer has gone unanswered or you don't have the things of life you think you should enjoy. Does this make you question if God exists?

The Big Play

Perhaps you have questions like Adam did. Do you believe and trust in God, or do you doubt His promises? Are you searching for the truth? Hopefully, you are close to making a decision to follow Christ and find His plan for you. If so, this is an exciting time for you as you consider giving your heart to the Lord.

The Coach's Corner

Once you make that choice to ask Jesus into your heart, you will look back and wonder why it took you so long. It's like getting on a roller coaster for the first time. At first, you are scared, but after it's over, you want to get back and ride it again right away. It's the same way with God. After you give Him control of your life, you'll enjoy the ride more. Don't just go through the motions. Get on the ride and have fun.

> *But my life is worth nothing to me unless I use it for finishing the work assigned me by the Lord Jesus—the work of telling others the Good News about the wonderful grace of God.*
> —Acts 20:24

CHAPTER 36
TAKE A KNEE BEFORE GOD

Adam Vinatieri
NFL Kicker

There has been a lot of discussion and controversy about taking a knee during the national anthem over the past few years. But due to our nation's freedoms, for the most part, players have been able to make their own personal choices as to whether or not they stood or kneeled.

But someday, all will kneel before the Lord with no exceptions. We will all have to answer in judgment to the King of Kings and Lord of Lords.

Adam has no problem in taking a knee before Christ. In fact, that's how he likes to begin each day.

"That's a great place to start your life and your day," he said. "It's been a wonderful life . . . and it all started with me on my knees."

Adam has gone to his knees many times over the years in honor of God.

One such time was during the NFL draft, when no teams picked him to join their roster. Can you imagine that no one wanted him?

"I just remember dropping to my knees and asking God for direction. I prayed, 'If this is what you want me to do, let's go. If not, lead me in another direction,'" he said.

Adam was willing to walk away from football if God wanted. He was ready. He even thought about enrolling in medical school.

But the Lord opened a door for him to play in the World League of American Football.

Soon, the New England Patriots found him, and the rest is history. Adam is regarded as one of the best kickers ever to play in the NFL.

His journey to stardom began on his knees in prayer. He always gives thanks to the Master for guiding his life.

"No matter if I have a tough day or not, my kids come running to me and give me a big hug. There's nothing better than that. It makes the day worthwhile and makes me forget about any problems," he said. "I get out of the way and let Him do the planning."

The Big Moment

Do you need the Lord to help you chart the course for your life? Maybe you are trying to decide which sport to play or what school to attend. You might be looking for a church or asking God to lead you to the right person to date. These are big decisions, and you don't want to screw things up.

The Big Play

The best thing you can do is seek God's will. When Adam was overlooked in the NFL draft, he poured his heart out to the Lord and pleaded for wisdom. God delivered. Don't get in the way of God's plans. Turn your future over to Him and walk through the doors He opens for you.

The Coach's Corner

It's a tough situation when your goals don't match up with God's plan for your life. This is why it's crucial to pray and even fast about big choices. Don't rush into anything, and don't try to talk your heavenly father into changing His mind. When He opens the door, follow the path He provides. Adam did, and it took him to great accomplishments in the NFL.

"As surely as I live," says the LORD, "every knee will bend to me, and every tongue will declare allegiance to God."

—Romans 14:11

CHAPTER 37
IN GOD'S TIMING

Andrew McCutchen
MLB Outfielder

Romans 8:28 is Andrew's favorite verse. It's simple and to the point, much like him.

The verse says, "And we know that God causes everything to work together for the good of those who love God and are called according to his purpose for them."

His gritty style of play and coming through when it counts has earned him the nickname "Cutch."

In 2009, he was called up to the Big Leagues and took the game by storm. Since then, he has experienced highs and lows.

Cutch made several All-Star teams, won a few Silver Slugger Awards, and was named the National League MVP in 2013.

A few years later he struggled when he posted the lowest batting average of his career in 2016. Then he was traded.

But the one constant in his life has been God's love.

"The plan of God is the plan of God," he stated. "You have to just trust in what He has planned for you—just continue that journey and keep on the road, stay positive, and find joy in the midst of the struggles."

Challenges have come and gone, but the Lord's love for him has never changed.

Andrew is aware that no matter how he performs on the field, or how bad things might get off the field, the Master is in control of everything.

"I would not be here without Him. He has given me so many blessings and opportunities I don't deserve," he said.

The Big Moment

Have you ever felt like you were on top of the world? Maybe you passed a tough exam and you're elated that your hours of study paid off. Then the very next day, you strike out four times in a row, and the coach sends you to the bench.

The Big Play

Perspective is a wonderful thing, but it's hard to have at times. If you're not careful, you can be on the mountain one day, and in the valley the next. But you need to know that without a shadow of a doubt, God loves you and has a plan for your life. He wants you to have peace and joy. When things don't go the way you want, remember that He has your back, and don't take your disappointments out on your friends, family, or teammates.

The Coach's Corner

Performing well on the field is important, but not as valuable as the future God is planning for you. At the end of the day, when you lay your head on your pillow, you can put aside the strikeouts and the A+ you received on your exam and be ready for what Christ has in store.

> *But blessed are those who trust in the LORD*
>   *and have made the LORD their hope and confidence.*
> *They are like trees planted along a riverbank,*
>   *with roots that reach deep into the water.*
> *Such trees are not bothered by the heat*
>   *or worried by long months of drought.*
> *Their leaves stay green,*
>   *and they never stop producing fruit.*
>
>   —Jeremiah 17:7–8

CHAPTER 38
TELL ALL YOUR FRIENDS

Anthony Muñoz
Hall of Fame NFL Tackle

Can you believe that NFL Hall of Famer Anthony Muñoz was never presented with the message of the gospel of Jesus Christ until he was a college student?

It's true.

The Cincinnati Bengals legend was a freshman at the University of Southern California when he first heard about the love of Jesus.

"I never heard about Christ until I went to college," he said. "And once I heard about it, I knew I wanted to live for the Lord."

Anthony was a popular athlete in high school, and many recruiters and scouts tried to get him to attend their colleges.

But he eventually chose USC where he played football and baseball. Then he went on to play in the NFL and was inducted into the Pro Football Hall of Fame in 1998.

It was during his freshman year at college that a staff member with Campus Crusade for Christ presented the wonderful and good news of God's love to him.

"I sat down with them one day, and he started to ask me questions," Anthony said. "He asked me about how my freshman year was going and about my grades and football."

Then he asked about his spiritual life.

"I said it was okay, but it was nonexistent," Anthony said. "I didn't know what he was talking about."

Soon others started to witness to him and told him about the plan of salvation.

"I started to think everyone was ganging up on me, because they were coming at me from all directions," he said with a laugh.

Six months after he was married in 1978, Anthony and his wife both gave their hearts to the Lord.

"God used so many people to get to me," he said. "That's why I always talk about His mercy on me and His greatness. I want everyone to have the same Lord."

The Big Moment

Do you let opportunities go by without telling your friends about the God you serve? Are you embarrassed or scared to reveal the love of Christ to your friends? Maybe you have a fear of being labeled and you step back from chances to share the gospel out of fear of being ridiculed.

The Big Play

You don't have to be a bully when you witness to your friends about why you are a Christian. You can just have a simple conversation. A friend might ask:

"How was your weekend?"

"It was great—I went to an outing with our youth group and had a wonderful time. If you ever want to go, let me know. I think you would like it."

It's that simple. No pressure. No guilt or shame. You can use a simple invitation that might open the door to talk more about God's love.

The Coach's Corner

Starting a discussion about serving Christ can be life changing. A staffer at college talked to Anthony about his faith, and he and his wife became Christians and now live a fantastic life.

Don't wait too long to share the gospel with your friends.

> *When we get together, I want to encourage you in your faith, but I also want to be encouraged by yours.*
>
> —Romans 1:12

CHAPTER 39
LESSONS LEARNED

Mike Sarbaugh
MLB Base Coach

Do you react well when there is little time to think or prepare? Can you make a decision in a split second when the game is on the line?

As a third-base coach in the MLB, Mike faces tough decisions every game. His choices to send a runner home or hold him at third have determined the outcome of games.

You might not think it's that tough, but it is. There is a lot of pressure riding on his judgment call.

"You just have to recognize the situation and rely on your gut and from research you do on players," he said. "You have to know the arm strength of an outfielder, if he can make the throw to home, and I have to know our players and how fast they are. Plus, I have to be aware of the situation at the moment."

When the runners cross home plate safely, he has made the right call. But if the runner is thrown out, then it falls back on him.

"Sometimes I make mistakes," he said. "Once that decision has been made, I can't go back and redo it. I have to live with the outcome."

The same applies to your daily walk.

You make decisions every day as part of life. What to wear. What to eat. Whether or not to listen to your parents or coaches.

A split-second decision can destroy your reputation and change your life.

You will face temptations from the enemy of the other team all the time. A "friend" might ask you to take a smoke, or a drink of alcohol.

Choices have consequences. And when you choose to participate in sin, it will take you much farther than you had planned. This might not happen immediately, but it definitely leads to a slow fade.

You will reap what you sow. Decisions lead to consequences.

Make the right ones.

The Big Moment

Perhaps you go to church and have earned a solid reputation. You play by the rules at home, school, and on the ball field. But the devil knows this and will try to fire a fast ball past you and strike you out. He might use a friend to tempt you into cheating on a test or lure you into trying something bad "just once." Will you watch the third base coach to see if he waves you into home?

The Big Play

One wrong decision can result in a lifetime of problems. You may think it will never happen to you, but it only takes one wrong decision to change your life. This is why you need to be faithful to church and surround yourself with a solid support system of Christian friends and family who love you.

The Coach's Corner

If you have second thoughts about a decision, the odds are that you should not do it. If a red flag is raised, take note. Your gut instinct is a wonderful gauge. Seek God in prayer, and ask Him to always help you to do the right thing.

He grants a treasure of common sense to the honest.
 He is a shield to those who walk with integrity.
                                                —Proverbs 2:7

CHAPTER 40
MAKE THE COMEBACK

Chad Pennington
NFL Quarterback

If you play sports, you are likely to be injured at one time or another.

If you're lucky, you might just get minor cuts or bruises, but you could also experience a more serious injury that keeps you off the field of play for a while.

An injury can heal quickly, or it can take months or years to recover after a surgery.

Be prepared because you will get hurt.

Chad knows something about bumps and bruises.

In fact, he won the NFL Comeback Player of the Year TWO times, which is rare.

The Marshall University alum won it the first time in 2006 when he led the New York Jets to a 10-6 season and their first playoff appearance in years. This was after he had two surgeries in 2005 to repair his throwing shoulder.

"That felt good to be recognized for all the hard work and dedication I put in to come back," he said. "That meant a lot."

The next year he suffered a serious high-ankle injury, and in 2008, he landed a spot with the Miami Dolphins.

He had an outstanding season and led the NFL in passing completion percentage (67.4) and posted a passer rating of 97.4. He guided the Dolphins to an 11-5 record, threw for 3,500 yards, and finished second in the MVP voting. He won the comeback title a second time.

His determination showed that he was able to bounce back after serious injuries. He put in the time and hard work to reach the milestone.

"I don't think the appreciation level ever changes, you just have to understand that there's always going to be highs and lows," he said. "And it's always to the extreme, because the middle of the road doesn't sail, and it's not exciting. The extremes—that's what's exciting, and that is what everybody leans on."

Life will also cause you some injuries. Will you be able to recover?

The Big Moment

Maybe a friend told a lie about you that damaged your reputation. Or perhaps you have been betrayed by someone close to you and left with some emotional scars. No matter what happened or who did it, you may have drifted in your spiritual walk with the Lord. Never let what someone else does to you injure your relationship with God.

The Big Play

This is a hard lesson, but there will be people you count on who will let you down in life. Some may cause spiritual damage to you. Chad was able to come back from not one, but two major injuries to lead two different teams to the post season. When he was benched in New York, he felt betrayed, but he kept working hard. He could have quit or retired, but he knew he had more to offer. And so do you.

The Coach's Corner

The best way to heal from the hurt is to go deeper in the Word of God. Stay faithful to God, and find peace and joy through fellowship with your church family. Don't judge others and don't turn away from those who love you. Let it go, forgive, and go on to the next game. Get up, dust off the dirt, and get back on the field.

> *The godly may trip seven times, but they will get up again.*
> *But one disaster is enough to overthrow the wicked.*
> —Proverbs 24:16

CHAPTER 41
GOD WILL BE THERE FOR YOU

Cody Allen
MLB Pitcher

At some point in your life, you will have to make the decision to accept God's plan of salvation or ignore it.

If you have already made a commitment to serve the Lord, then you are on the winning team.

It doesn't matter if you have been raised in church or not, sooner or later you have to choose. You can't ride into heaven on the faith of your parents.

Cody grew up in church where he learned right from wrong. He enjoyed being a part of the congregation and felt safe.

But when he was in the eighth grade, he felt something different. Conviction.

He knew that his upbringing would not be enough to make it to heaven, and he made the choice to accept Jesus into his heart.

"It wasn't so much it was the right thing to do," he said. "I felt real conviction, and I wanted to live a life of integrity."

Deep down, he knew his parents would always love him no matter what, but he knew it was the best move for him. He saw the benefits of living for the Lord.

"I wanted to start living right because God wanted me to," he added. "It wasn't because I was raised in church. I was exposed to church, but I was the one who decided to live for the Lord."

And even though Cody made it to the MLB, he still faced everyday problems like anyone else. But he doesn't let that bother him because he knows the Lord is always there for him.

"God is not going to turn his head and just let us go off and die," he said. "He has told me that He will take care of me, and I trust Him."

Have you made the decision to follow Christ?

The Big Moment

Maybe you were raised in church like Cody. You attend Sunday school and youth group and never get into trouble. That's fantastic. But are you a Christian?

The Big Play

Learning about God, attending church, and living the right way is awesome, but none of these things are enough to get you into heaven. If you want to go there, you must accept God's plan of salvation and live a holy life. Can you do this in front of your friends at school? Absolutely. Will you have a problem-free life? No. But you will have peace and joy in your heart instead of pain and misery.

The Coach's Corner

Your best life is to be a believer and follow the Lord Jesus Christ. It's easy to make this choice. Pray and ask the Lord to forgive you of your sins and commit to live according to His plan. Ask Him to live in your heart and lead you through life's journey. Find a church to attend, pray, and read your Bible every day. Having God on your side will give you the strength you need when hard times come to help get you back in the game.

And now, just as you accepted Christ Jesus as your Lord, you must continue to follow him.

—Colossians 2:6

CHAPTER 42
IT'S OKAY TO SPEAK OUT

Kurt Warner
Hall of Fame NFL Quarterback

Making a bold statement or a prediction can put you in a sticky situation—especially when the outcome has yet to be decided.

It's always the best judgment to let your actions speak for themselves and refrain from verbal confrontation when it comes to competition.

I remember back when I was playing high school football and our local sportswriters all predicted that my team would be defeated by the frontrunner at the time. We were in last place in the conference at that time, and one sportswriter said the other team was "tougher" than we were.

That fired up our coach, and in turn, he motivated us to go out and win. We pulled off the upset.

Words can persuade and influence.

Kurt Warner knows all about this and gave the best example when he proclaimed his love for the Lord on the biggest stage in the world.

After his Rams won Super Bowl XXXIV in 2000, he was on national television during the celebration and gave glory and honor to Jesus Christ. The crowd loved his words.

"I think one of the greatest moves I ever made was when I professed Jesus on the podium after I won the Super Bowl," he said. "Because now, everyone knows about my faith."

Many fans knew he was a good guy, but his public announcement sealed the deal.

When he witnessed to millions of television viewers and to the fans in the stands, he knew he had to live up to his testimony.

"When I did that and thanked Jesus, it pushed me to be more accountable with my faith and turned out to be the greatest blessing I've enjoyed," he added. "Everyone knows that I'm a Christian, and I love that."

Have you had an opportunity to tell others that you follow Christ? Would you do what Kurt did?

The Big Moment

The league championship game is on the line, and your team pulls off the upset. You play a big part in the game, and a huge celebration ensues. Later in the locker room, some sports writers and radio broadcasters want to talk to you about what the win means for the team. This gives you the opportunity to thank God live on the air and tell everyone who reads the news articles about your faith. Will you do it?

The Big Play

You may never be on a stage with a Super Bowl trophy in your hands in front of millions of people when you proclaim God's love, but you might. Jump at any chance you get to tell others about the Lord you serve. You might tell a few people attending your birthday or graduation party, or you might proclaim it when you sign your letter of intent to play college athletics. Take advantage of all opportunities to witness to others about the love of God.

The Coach's Corner

There are many ways to tell others about the grace of Christ. You can post on social media, testify in youth group settings, or even at a pep rally. There are no limits to your boldness.

> *Boldly proclaiming the Kingdom of God and teaching about the Lord Jesus Christ. And no one tried to stop him.*
>
> —Acts 28:21

CHAPTER 43
MAKE THE IMPACT PLAY

Blaine Boyer
MLB Pitcher

Many people can make an impact on your life.

It might be a teacher, coach, player, or even a Sunday school teacher or pastor.

But could someone you don't know make a difference in your life? This happened to Blaine.

He was in high school and hanging out with some friends at a lake house by a campfire.

He described himself as a "punk kid" and a "disaster of an individual" at the time. His buddy's grandmother came out to visit the crew at the fire, and soon he found himself alone with the elderly lady, engaged in conversation.

She presented the gospel to him in such a way he had to listen. Blaine was captivated by her divine words of wisdom.

"She talked to me out of love and from the goodness of her heart," Blaine said. "She just told me the truth about what would happen to me if I didn't get saved.

"She told me where I was headed, and I just felt that Jesus used her to zero right into my heart," he said. "It was so real—it was like God was right there. He was locked in on my heart, and that's when things started to change for me."

That's where Blaine's journey with faith started.

"I'm so thankful for that night many years ago and for her faith and obedience to share the story with me," he said. "She cared about me, even though she really didn't know me. That has always been in the back of my mind, and I try to show the same love for everyone."

Can you influence someone like that?

The Big Moment

Is God important enough in your life that you would share the plan of salvation with someone you don't know well? Granted, the lady was experienced and mature. But age does not disqualify you from sharing the gospel. If you're around the campfire with friends and someone there needs to hear about God's grace, will you step up to the plate?

The Big Play

There are good and bad ways to share the news of God with others. Let the Holy Spirit guide you and help you realize when the opportunity presents itself. Show humbleness and compassion, not judgment—that is God's role. A simple offer to pray with them might be just what they are looking for in a friend. Maybe you could invite them to church or Sunday school where they will hear the Gospel. Stay in touch and always let them know you are there for them. Live a godly life in front of them. Be a teammate.

The Coach's Corner

The conversation between Blaine and his friend's grandmother changed his life forever. You can make a similar impact. But you must prepare yourself daily for this moment. Pray, read the Word, and ask God to put someone in your life whom you can be a witness to. Just as you practice fielding and hitting, you can also perfect the art of being a good witness.

> *Come and listen, all you who fear God,*
> *and I will tell you what he did for me.*
>
> —Psalm 66:16

CHAPTER 44
TACKLE PERSONAL STRUGGLES

Tom Lamphere
NFL Chaplain

Personal challenges often are magnified for a teenager.

A personal issue can distract you from a goal and turn you in a different direction. One bad choice can set you back years if you are not careful.

Mistakes will be made. You may also experience tragedies.

I lost my father when I still needed him to help me learn. His death forced me to grow up fast, and I had to figure things out on my own.

Life can be a struggle.

Tom, as a team chaplain, has seen his share of players who deal with conflict.

Just because professional athletes have a lot of money and fame, they are not excluded from making mistakes that can damage their reputations or even take their lives.

"All of us will go through difficult times and face personal turmoil," he said. "But how do we handle it? I think when we open up as coaches and players, it helps to heal or get through a challenge."

When a player gets into trouble, a lot of people find out about it thanks to the twenty-four-hour news cycle. And the problem really blows up if that person has previously proclaimed faith in God.

"When people are in the spotlight and they profess Christianity, everyone watches to see how they respond to this type of event," he said. "People watch to see how they get through, and it's always through the grace of God."

When you are a professing Christian and you make a moral mistake, you will be under a public microscope. People expect more from you as a believer.

The devil wants to see you fail, and when you choose to follow the Lord, you will have a target on your back, and the forces of evil will try to make a direct hit to cause you damage.

You have a lot of choices as a kid. Drugs. Alcohol. Cigarettes. Pornography. None of these things will make you a better person or athlete.

Strive to be an athlete who walks with Christ. Be someone whom others look up to and count on to be a godly example.

The Big Moment

After a big win, how do you celebrate by giving your teammates credit? How do you prepare for a big test? Do you try to cheat on the exam? You have a lot at stake as an athlete, and a lot of eyes are on you.

The Big Play

Always do your best. If it's good enough for the win, that's fantastic. If your team comes up short even when you put forth your best effort, it's okay. If you prepare for the test and pass, then you can reap the rewards. However, if you are overwhelmed, then you know where you came up short and can try harder in the future.

The Coach's Corner

Don't look at the size of your problem but focus on the Lord's power. A wall can seem too high to climb at times, or the valley can be too low to cross. But the Master promised to never leave you nor forsake you, so look to Him for help.

Give all your worries and cares to God, for he cares about you.
—1 Peter 5:7

CHAPTER 45
CHOOSE YOUR FRIENDS WISELY

Mike Matheny
MLB Manager

Even at a young age, it's never too early to select great friends.

You will be linked to whomever you hang out with. Your choice of friends will say a lot about you and will set the stage for your future.

Your selection can also damage your reputation. If you spend your time with those who break rules or disobey authority, then you will be known for that too.

Mike Matheny was taught early in life about accountability and responsibility.

As a manager in the MLB, he was responsible for putting a winning team on the field. And as a Christian, he was accountable to the Lord and his family.

To help him achieve success in both arenas, he surrounded himself with good people.

"I personally have a board of directors that I can lean on," Mike said. "They have been there for me as far as spiritual growth and leadership."

When you have people in your life who hold you responsible, it makes you want to do the right thing all the time.

A buddy will let you do anything, but a friend will tell you when you are making a mistake.

"There is always room to grow as a Christian, and we all want to do our best," he said, "I have people with me who watch me, and more importantly it's who lives within me that watches me. I need to stay sharp because there is an enemy, and I need all the help I can get."

After I spoke with Mike, I copied his plan and formed my own group of friends whom I have challenged to hold me accountable. I appreciate them, and they know we are all in this together. They are true friends.

The Big Moment

A small group of teenagers who have a reputation of getting into trouble has asked you to hang out with them. They openly show disrespect for authority. They want you to be a part of their group because you have a solid reputation. What do you do?

The Big Play

The best thing to do is to be polite and tell them you are busy with schoolwork and practice when they invite you to their parties. Turn the tables and invite them to church, or to a youth outing. Be a witness to them and do not look down on them. Hold yourself to a higher standard and draw a line in the sand to do what's right.

The Coach's Corner

Find people who inspire you to do better. Choose friends you can trust. If you're a male, you need other males on your board—brothers in Christ who have your best interests at heart. I try to hold conference calls or Zoom meetings with my board. You can meet at the library or have a Bible study after practice. The key is to have a strong lineup of support.

> *I also tell you this: If two of you agree here on earth concerning anything you ask, my Father in heaven will do it for you.*
> —Matthew 18:19

CHAPTER 46
PUT IT DOWN IN WORDS

Morgan Cox
NFL Long Snapper

Morgan Cox does not get a lot of attention for his job, unless he makes a mistake.

He is a long snapper on special teams in the NFL and must be ready to perform at all times.

Quarterbacks make several throws throughout a game while the long snapper gets only a few shots to succeed.

Morgan has no room or time for errors. If he makes a bad snap, then the team could lose the game.

He doesn't get a lot of publicity, and that's okay with him. But he is always prepared and practices his craft daily.

He took the same approach when he found out that he was going to be a dad.

Morgan and his wife started to read the Word of God together each day and made notes for their son to read when he was older. They wrote down lessons and take-aways from what they read together for their child to treasure one day.

Morgan's parents did the same thing for him.

"What they did for me helped me to stay grounded in my faith," he said. "I had the idea to do this while Daniel was still in the womb.

"My goal is to be a man of God for him and let him see what's really important," he said. "I can be accountable to him, and keeping a journal helps me in that goal."

Taking notes and writing down your thoughts on paper can be a comfort to you and help you express yourself.

The Big Moment

Perhaps you have a younger sibling or maybe your parents are expecting. You can do that same thing Morgan did and leave a gift for your little brother or sister. Or perhaps you can do something similar for your parents or grandparents. They would love and treasure a note from you telling them what they mean to you and how much you love them.

The Big Play

It doesn't take long to put your words down on paper. Take a few moments each week to write down something special for your parents, grandparents, or siblings to read later. You can make it a Christmas project and work on it all year long. What a blessing that would be.

The Coach's Corner

When you take time to do something special like this, it's precious to the person who receives the gift. In your daily devotions, write down your thoughts about your family and what they mean to you. Or you can journal each day about how good God has been to you. Make out a prayer list, and take joy in crossing a line through the ones that God

answers. You can also put down your innermost feelings
for your future partner to read and cherish. Think about
starting a journal or even a project for your parents for a
birthday or holiday gift. This would be worth more to them
than any Super Bowl ring you might win.

Good people leave an inheritance to their grandchildren,
but the sinner's wealth passes to the godly.

—Proverbs 13:22

CHAPTER 47
LEAD THE WAY

Tim Martin
MLB Scout

After Tim's future in the MLB as a pitcher was cut short after surgery, he became bitter.

He loved playing and watching baseball.

But after he was released from the Pirates organization, he turned his back on the sport.

A decade later, he was asked to coach his high school alma mater. But he still didn't like the game much, and his frustrations mounted.

"I'd come home after a big win and just be bent out of shape and mad," he said. "I'd find something small and let it eat at me. I never enjoyed the wins, because I wasn't happy inside.

Something was missing."

But what really bothered him was two of his players who would take the team out in left field before each game and pray with them.

They were the team leaders—not Tim.

"I'd sit there, and my blood would boil," he said. "We'd win the game, and I'd rip and yell at the kids for no reason." He was under conviction.

"I'd be in the dugout yelling at kids while those two guys were out there praying," he said. "They were setting a better example. I knew what I needed to do, but I fought it, because I didn't want to turn my life around."

In 2008, Tim gave his heart to the Lord. He found peace and enjoyed the game once again.

After that, he was the one who led the team in prayer. He set the example.

The Big Moment

Do your classmates or teammates look to you for leadership? Or do they think of you as a bitter person? What would you do if you were asked to lead your team in a prayer? Could you do it? Do they have enough confidence in your faith and witness?

The Big Play

If you are not a leader, then never try to force yourself into this role. Live your life by example, and others will see and follow. Stand on your convictions and never back down. When you live a true and faithful life for God, you are leading the way for all to see.

The Coach's Corner

There are a lot of things you can do to be a leader. Let others see you pray over your food or carry a Bible in your backpack. Ask the Lord for help to be a friend to all—even those who don't like you. Show compassion and love as much as you can, and be kind. Write your favorite verse on your glove or on your cleats. This could open the door to a conversation about salvation. You can do all these things and still be a fierce competitor on the field of play.

Don't let anyone think less of you because you are young. Be an example to all believers in what you say, in the way you live, in your love, your faith, and your purity.

—1 Timothy 4:12

CHAPTER 48
SING AWAY

Ben Utecht
NFL Tight End

Consistent injuries limited Ben's time as a professional football player.

He was a big tight end and won a Super Bowl with the Indianapolis Colts alongside Peyton Manning.

But he was prone to concussions. After his fifth one, he started to have issues with his memory.

He made the decision to retire at age thirty.

Ben loved to sing and always wanted to pursue music as a career. Soon after he retired, he recorded the song "You Will Always Be My Girls."

He dedicated the song to his wife and young girls in case his brain injuries made him forget who they were.

"I love music so much," he said. "I never prayed for success in music, but the Lord knew it was a passion of mine. My prayer was always, 'If it's something You want me to do, then bring the right people into my life.'"

He sang at a youth gathering, and Sandi Patty happened to be in the audience. She introduced him to Bill and Gloria Gaither, which led to his first album. He started to record more songs, and one of his albums was nominated for a Dove Award.

God had a plan to send Ben to Indianapolis for football and make a way for him to meet Sandi so his singing career could happen.

God is like that.

"If I had not gone to the Colts, I would never have sung at that rally and never met the people I did," he said. "God's timing and plan is amazing."

The Big Moment

Has an injury sidelined your dreams or aspirations? Maybe you worked hard all spring to play under the lights on Friday night. But you were sidelined and now have to sit the bench. Or maybe you have a health issue keeping you off the field. Has it ever occurred to you that God has bigger plans?

The Big Play

Disappointments are hard to accept, especially when you don't know if or when things will change. The last thing you want to hear is words like, "God knows best" or "It's in His timing." These statements can be tough to hear, but they are true.

The Coach's Corner

While you wait on God to reveal His plan, try to have a positive attitude and trust God's plan. Spend more time in prayer each day and ask for guidance. Praise your way through the storm, and prepare yourself for a big event from the Lord. Ben faced an uncertain future when he retired, but Christ had the plan just for him, which was revealed when Ben got out of the way and allowed the Lord to take control of the situation.

I know how to live on almost nothing or with everything. I have learned the secret of living in every situation, whether it is with a full stomach or empty, with plenty or little.
—Philippians 4:12

CHAPTER 49

WHAT IS YOUR WEAKNESS?

Adam Frazier
MLB Second Baseman

There is not one person who walks the earth who does not have a weakness.

For some, it might be French fries. Others might give in to ice cream or other sweets. These are harmless, although you might gain some weight.

But other temptations can pose a real danger.

Alcohol or drugs might trap you, as well as pornography or violent video games. Whatever pulls you away from God's love and takes over your mind can be a detriment.

Once you know your weakness, admit that you have a problem and ask God to help you combat it. You may want to talk with your parents, pastor, or even a counselor.

A few years ago, Adam told me that as a young baseball player, the opposite sex was a big distraction.

"Lusting is a big struggle for me at times," he said. "It's not easy but it's real. It's real for a lot of us playing this game."

Once the forces of evil know your weaknesses, they will use them to come at you hard. They will use social media, celebrities, and the media to glamorize sin to make it appealing. Don't fall for these tricks. Sin will always take you farther than you want to go.

It's vital to have a strong support system in place with real friends to help you.

"We try to be there for each other and watch out for one another," he said. "We hold each other accountable and that is a great thing. No one wants to see a teammate make a silly mistake."

If you are attracted to certain pictures or social media accounts, then unfollow or block them. If you follow certain people and hide this from your parents, chances are you should not be doing that in the first place.

Temptation will come at you every day. When you give in to it, then it becomes your weakness and can destroy you. When you turn it over to God, He will make you stronger and help you to fight Satan's attempts to take you down.

The Big Moment

Your "buddies" invite you out after a game and you accept, knowing you should not be with the crowd that will be there. They offer you some alcohol and pressure you into taking drugs. Then they pick up some members of the opposite sex and head to an unlit park. You know this is wrong.

The Big Play

This is real. What will you do? You must be strong and not worry about the pressures of social acceptance. Remember what God and your parents have taught you, and get out of the situation before law enforcement shows up. A criminal record will follow you for a long time and rearrange your future plans. If you're not driving, be sure to call someone to pick you up.

The Coach's Corner

Once you are able to figure out what makes you weak, you can better know how to protect yourself from bad things that captivate your thoughts. Adam knew what made him weak and had a support system in place to help keep him from making a bad choice. It's not a test. It's a major game with serious consequences. Don't get doubled off at second base.

> *The temptations in your life are no different from what others experience. And God is faithful. He will not allow the temptation to be more than you can stand. When you are tempted, he will show you a way out so that you can endure.*
>
> —1 Corinthians 10:13

CHAPTER 50
SACRIFICE EQUALS LOVE

Grant Haley
NFL Cornerback

If you are playing sports in junior high or high school, winning doesn't just happen out of the blue. It takes commitment, dedication, and sacrifice.

This is true at all levels.

Grant Haley would not be where he is today if it weren't for his mother—which is the case in many instances.

He was raised in a Christian home, but that did not mean he had an easy ride. He still had to work hard to prove himself on the field of play.

And his parents were right there all the way.

Grant gives a lot of credit to his mother, who took time to make sure he was prepared to play.

"I remember her driving me up and down the East Coast for football camps and how she took time out of her life for me," he said. "I'm talking about taking me to Florida, North Carolina, and Virginia—she really sacrificed for me."

And he acknowledges the commitment she made for him, which has guided him along the way.

"There is so much more in life and things that can affect your family every day," he added. "I have learned to have a positive outlook. I am growing into a man, and people watch me to see how I respond. I have to put forth a good image and live up to that image. People will depend on you whether you have a good day or a bad one. My mom was always positive—always. The outlook she has inspires me."

The Big Moment

When you make a big play or even make the team, do you reflect back on who helped you along the way? In the end, it's your talent and ability. But along the way, you must have had encouragement and support from people in your life who took care of you and pushed you to do better. Who washed your clothes? Who took you to practice? Who bought your equipment?

The Big Play

Parents, siblings, and other relatives and friends who helped you may not get recognition. It's a wonderful thing to be honored for your accomplishments. But always take time to show appreciation for those who helped you to be successful.

The Coach's Corner

It doesn't take much time to say "thank you" to your mom and dad and others who helped you along the way. Even if it's just two words. But you can find other ways to show them your gratitude. Send them a card with a handwritten note. Pick flowers for your mom, and save up to get your parents a gift card. Before you know it, time will be gone, and the opportunity to show people how you feel will be past. Show appreciation today.

> *All of this is for your benefit. And as God's grace reaches more and more people, there will be great thanksgiving, and God will receive more and more glory.*
> —2 Corinthians 4:15

CHAPTER 51
WHO ARE YOU?

Ben Zobrist
MLB MVP

Many young athletes in junior high and high school dream about hitting the home run in the bottom of the ninth inning to win the World Series.

There is nothing wrong with a goal like this, and it gives you something to shoot for.

Chances of this happening are slim—but not impossible.

Most athletes will seek employment after school and raise a family and try to excel in some other way.

High school or college sports will turn into summer, work, or church league competitions.

What you do in life does not define who you are. Only God does that.

You may not end up with the job you wanted, or you might encounter other disappointments, but these may all be part of God's plan for bigger and better things.

Ben is a professional baseball player who keeps life in perspective.

"Your life is not about what you can become—it's about who God says you are—based on what Christ has done," he said. "And through Christ you can be holy, pure, perfect, lovely, everything you want to be—not by your own effort but because Christ already accomplished that—it was all on your behalf—so you can be a child of God and a child of the King of Kings and Lord of Lords. That's an incredible feeling."

At times, like many ball players, he has fought with his own identity and does not like being put on a pedestal.

"Fighting the idolatry of putting my identity on what I do on a baseball field—taking joy in that—instead of taking joy in the fact that I'm a child of God," he said. "Winning games and awards is nice, but gaining my ultimate reward in heaven is what I really work for."

Ben wants to be recognized as much for his Christian witness as he is for his amazing feats on the field. For him, that would be true success.

"I don't have anything to boast about—there is nothing I can say that I've done—I can say my biggest success is that Christ did things through me—that's my success," he explains. "He has a hold of me, and I put my hands in His—I need Him every day . . . if people can identify Christ in me then I am being a successful Christian."

The Big Moment

Who are you if you don't make the team? Or what if you are not the star on the field? Perhaps you are not as involved in school activities and feel left out. But this doesn't define who you are.

The Big Play

You must realize that only God will define who you are in life. As long as you glorify Him in all you do, then you will be at peace. You might have to do a job you don't want for a while and resort to a backup plan, but that's okay as long as you allow the Lord to lead you. He will never take you down the wrong path.

The Coach's Corner

I've been there. I've struggled with difficult circumstances on the job that I did not like. At times I was frustrated, but I always knew deep down that God would take care of me. I've never been disappointed or let down. Trust God's plan for you.

My old self has been crucified with Christ. It is no longer I who live, but Christ lives in me. So I live in this earthly body by trusting in the Son of God, who loved me and gave himself for me.

—Galatians 2:20

CHAPTER 52
BE WHO GOD MADE YOU

Vinny Rey
NLF Linebacker

Being a young Christian is the best life, but it does have its challenges.

There is social pressure from all sides at times. How to dress. How to act. Conformity. Rules. This is a part of life. You want to fit in with the crowd, but God requires you to set yourself apart from the world.

Vinny faced the same dilemma. He was a believer and gave his heart to the Lord when he was seven years old.

He was raised to know the difference between right and wrong. But he had his own identity in Christ.

When he was fifteen, he was introduced to a new look and entertained a new perspective when the Cross Movement, a contemporary Christian hip-hop group, came to his church for a praise service. They made an impact on Vinny.

"It was really cool to hear them and meet them," he said. "I related to them and their message of Christ."

The group was not "traditional," but neither was Vinny.

"They spoke like I did, but they were different. They were mature Christians who I related with and looked up to and wanted to be like."

Right then and there, he knew he could serve the Lord and still be different. It was all okay. He could still dress like his friends and keep his style, but he did not have to attend wild parties to fit in. He could still be a witness in a different way and be bold.

He did not give in to society, yet he was still accepted. It was fantastic.

The Big Moment

Do you feel like you fit in? Do you need to fit in? Do you feel out of place for taking a stand for Christ? Have you been ridiculed for taking a stand for the Lord?

The Big Play

As a young man or woman, you see the need to be accepted by your peers but don't want to surrender to your convictions. You want to be an example, but you don't want to be a fuddy-duddy either. You want your friends to accept your beliefs and your style too. You never want to have a condemning attitude, yet you cannot give in to societal pressure. If you are invited to a party you know you should not attend, simply thank them for the invite and politely tell them you have other plans. Then return the favor and invite them to church.

The Coach's Corner

You can set yourself apart from the world and still fit in with your friends. You don't have to give in to what everyone else does. Follow your convictions and let the Lord and His spirit guide you. Never lower your standards for anyone. Once you let others know how you feel and be honest with them, they should respect that.

> *Don't copy the behavior and customs of this world, but let God transform you into a new person by changing the way you think. Then you will learn to know God's will for you, which is good and pleasing and perfect.*
>
> —Romans 12:2

If you enjoyed this book, will you consider sharing the message with others?

Let us know your thoughts. You can let the author know by visiting or sharing a photo of the cover on our social media pages or leaving a review at a retailer's site. All of it helps us get the message out!

Email: info@ironstreammedia.com

  @ironstreammedia

———————

Brookstone Publishing Group, Iron Stream, Iron Stream Fiction, Iron Stream Harambee, Iron Stream Kids, and Life Bible Study are imprints of Iron Stream Media, which derives its name from Proverbs 27:17, "As iron sharpens iron, so one person sharpens another." This sharpening describes the process of discipleship, one to another. With this in mind, Iron Stream Media provides a variety of solutions for churches, ministry leaders, and nonprofits ranging from in-depth Bible study curriculum and Christian book publishing to custom publishing and consultative services.

For more information on ISM and its imprints, please visit IronStreamMedia.com

Made in United States
Troutdale, OR
06/19/2023

10690200R00100